LENDING POLICY
IF YOU DAMAGE OR LOSE THIS BOOK YOU
WILL BE CHARGED FOR ITS REPLACEMENT.
FAILURE TO PAY AFFECTS REGISTRATION,
TRANSCRIPTS, AND LIBRARY PRIVILEGES.

You Can Be a Machinist

Arthur Liebers
You Can Be a Machinist

Illustrated with photographs

Lothrop, Lee & Shepard Company • New York

Vocations in Trades books by Arthur Liebers

YOU CAN BE A CARPENTER
YOU CAN BE A PLUMBER
YOU CAN BE AN ELECTRICIAN
YOU CAN BE A MECHANIC
YOU CAN BE A MACHINIST

Title page photograph:

This huge forming press shows how important machinists are to our country's industry. Machinists produced the parts that were assembled to make this machine. Now, other machinists use it to produce a steady flow of shaped metal parts for other types of machinery.

(*American Machinist Magazine photo*)

1   2   3   4   5   79   78   77   76   75

Library of Congress Cataloging in Publication Data

Liebers, Arthur (date)
    You can be a machinist.

    (His Vocations in trades)
    Includes index.
    SUMMARY: A guide to becoming a machinist, including information on the kinds of work, advantages and disadvantages of the career, apprenticeship and training, aptitude tests, and more.
    1. Machine shops—Vocational guidance—Juvenile literature. [1. Machine shops—Vocational guidance.   2. Vocational guidance]   I. Title.
TJ1125.L53   621.7'5   75-16390
ISBN 0-688-41719-1
ISBN 0-688-51719-6 lib. bdg.

Contents

Acknowledgments

The author wishes to thank the trade associations, companies in the field and government agencies whose cooperation made this book possible. The editorial staff of *American Machinist,* a McGraw-Hill publication, was a source of valuable information and illustrations.

Among those who are owed special thanks for their contributions are: John E. Williams, Manager, Communications, The National Tool, Die & Precision Machining Association; Charles Pollock, Public Relations Director, National Machine Tool Builders' Association; Byron L. Friend, President, Vocational Films; Ina Geller, Communications Officer, Pierce College; F. H. Clarkson, Jr., Promotion Manager, The L. S. Starrett Company; and Ms. Anna C. Urband, Media Services Branch, U. S. Navy Office of Information.

Bill Donnelly of the Grumman Aerospace Corporation was most helpful in sharing his thirty-two years of experience as a machinist with the author.

The Psychological Corporation of New York City allowed use of their copyrighted test materials, and various offices of the State Employment Service were most cooperative.

Other credits appear in the text and captions.

1/The Work
of the Machinist

If you have a good head for math, enjoy working with your hands, and get a kick out of something you have made yourself, you may find a satisfying career as a machinist.

Almost every product made by American industry contains metal parts or is manufactured by machines made up of many metal parts. Machinists, or machining workers as they are sometimes called, have two important functions:

1. They create the machines that produce the thousands of items that we all use every year;

2. They operate the machines that turn out these parts. This may seem a bit confusing, but it will clear up as you read this book.

A Big Work Force In thinking about any future career, one important fact to consider is whether you will be able to find a job in that line of work. Machining workers make up one of the largest working groups in the country. About a million and a quarter men and women are employed as machinists, tool and die makers, instrument makers, machine tool operators, and setup operators. With that large a work force, there are constant openings to replace

The many different objects in this photo may give you an idea of the products turned out by machinists. Even the largest must be accurate to within thousandths of an inch.

(Moog Incorporated photo)

retiring workers and to fill new jobs in the field.

During a recent period of general unemployment, the manager of a state employment office told this author, "If a skilled machinist walks into my office on Friday, I can have him at work Monday morning."

At the same time, an employment interviewer at another state employment office said, "For six months we have been trying to find a multiple-spindle drill press setup operator for fifteen thousand dollars a year, and haven't succeeded."

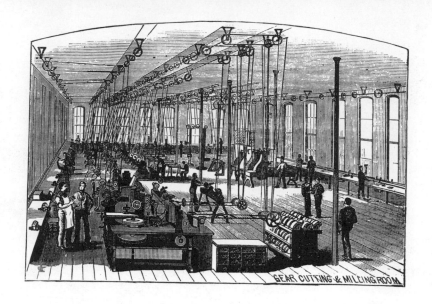

The work of the machinist has changed over the years. This sketch of a gear cutting and milling room was made about a hundred years ago. Power for the machines came from the overhead pulleys, which controlled the speed and power of the operations.

(Brown & Sharpe Manufacturing Company photo)

What They Do   The principal work of most machinists and machining workers is to operate machine tools. A **machine tool** is a stationary machine, driven by power, that holds both the piece of metal to be shaped and a cutting instrument or "tool," and brings them together so that the metal is cut to the desired shape and size. In some machines, the cutting tool is moved and the metal is held stationary; in others, the metal is moved against a stationary tool.

The most common types of machine tools are lathes, grinding machines, drilling and boring machines, milling machines, shapers, broachers, and

10

planers. (You will find out more about them in later chapters.)

Lathes turn and shape metal against a sharp cutting tool. Grinding machines smooth metal parts by using power-driven abrasive wheels. Drilling machines make holes in metal. Boring machines enlarge holes already drilled. Milling machines cut or remove excess metal with tools that have several cutting edges. Shapers, planers, and broachers are machine tools that produce flat surfaces.

If you are interested in the type of work that is moving ahead with modern science, you will find it in the machining industry. In the past few years

Space-age Changes

In this modern plant, tape-controlled machines turn out the work you can see on tables behind the operators.

(*Moog Incorporated photo*)

An example of precision work. When these two parts are assembled, they must fit perfectly. A skilled machinist who saw this picture said it was a fairly simple operation to produce such units.

(Kennametal photo)

many new metal-shaping techniques have been developed. For example, metal can now be shaped using chemicals, electricity, magnetism, sound, light, and liquids under controlled conditions.

Another big change in the industry has been the development of what is called **numerical control.** That is the operation of machine tools by coded tapes and computers. This has created many new jobs for programmers, who prepare the tapes that feed instructions into the machines, and technicians, to operate and service the NC equipment.

Precision, Precision, Precision

Precision is the goal in most machining work. Motors and machines—and a good example is the typewriter being used to write this book—are made of metal parts. The parts must be made to precise dimensions so that they will be interchangeable and can be readily assembled in mass production.

Metal parts are sometimes machined to **toler-**

ances, or limits, of ten millionths of an inch. Machining workers follow directions from drawings or blueprints on which the exact dimensions of the finished part are specified. Machining workers frequently use micrometers and other precision measuring instruments to check the accuracy of their work against the required specifications.

In addition to operating the machine tools, skilled tool and die makers, instrument makers, and machinists spend much of their time doing precision hand work such as laying out and assembling metal parts.

After the separate parts have been machined, they use files, scrapers, emery cloths, and other

The machine does not work by itself. Here the machinist is checking the finished work to be sure it meets specifications.

(Jones & Lamson photo)

small hand tools to file, scrape, and polish the parts for exact fit in the final assembly.

The Kinds of Machinists

All-around machinists are the most highly skilled workers, who can operate most types of machine tools. **Machine tool operators** commonly operate only one kind of machine tool. **Tool and die makers** specialize in making dies for use with presses and die-casting machines, devices to guide drills into metal, and special gages to determine whether the work meets the required specifications. **Instrument makers** use machine tools to produce highly accurate instrument parts made of metal or other materials. **Setup** workers adjust machine tools so that less skilled workers can run the machines. (Later in this chapter we will take a closer look at what each of these workers in the machining industry does.)

Some Plus and Some Minus Features

There is no such thing as a perfect job. All jobs have advantages and drawbacks. Machining work can be tedious at times. When machine tools are in operation, continuous attention is required, especially on simple, mass-production jobs. Also, working to such high precision standards can be a strain on the nerves and eyes. On the other hand, where the job is varied and complex and the standards of accuracy high, you can experience the satisfaction that comes to a capable and conscientious craftsman, and you are working in a field where you can see and admire what you have helped to create.

14

Many machinists work with wood as well as metal. These operators are trimming heavy laminated wood.

(*Kennametal photo*)

There is a certain element of danger in working around high-speed machine tools and sharp cutting instruments. But most machine shops are relatively clean and well-lighted, and the federal government has set rigid requirements for safety devices on machines to reduce the possibility of injury to workers. Persons working around machine tools are prohibited from wearing loose-fitting clothing, and in most shops safety glasses and other protective equipment are required.

Machining work is not usually physically strenuous. The machine tools do the actual cutting while the machining workers set the machines, watch the controls, and check the accuracy of the work. However, this type of work requires you to stand most of the day and move about frequently.

What About Advancement?

If you have ambitions to get ahead, there are opportunities in machining work. One example is **shop supervisors**, who have prestige in the craft and high earnings. Some experienced workers take specialized training to become **programmers**, who prepare the tapes that are used to operate the numerically controlled machines. Tool and die makers can advance to technical positions such as **tool and die designer** or **instrument technician.**

Also, a large part of the machining industry consists of small shops owned by former machining workers who set out on their own or with a partner to open their own tool and die shops or machine shops. Many that started as a one- or two-person operation have expanded to become fairly large and profitable plants.

Earnings

The satisfaction you could find in your work is important in choosing your future career. Equally important is the subject of money. What does that career offer in terms of lifetime earnings?

A few years ago, the U. S. Bureau of Labor Statistics, a government agency, made a study of twenty-six occupations on the basis of life earnings. Machinists were found to be among the top ten occupations when it comes to earnings. Some

The tape-editor looks pretty much like any typewriter, but it is a very special machine designed to turn out the tape you see at the left. That tape will give directions to the machine in the shop. (*Jones & Lamson photo*)

others in the top group were dentists, electrical and mechanical engineers, physicians and surgeons, manufacturing executives, civil and stationary engineers, and personnel and labor relations workers. In that group, machinists ranked seventh, putting them in good company money-wise.

Another feature to consider in choosing a trade is the regularity of employment, which affects the amount of money you could expect to earn each year. Another government study, this one by the U. S. Census Bureau, gathered information on the actual weeks worked during a year by different occupational groups. It was found that eighty-two percent of the machinists worked between fifty and fifty-two weeks a year. For a contrast, it was found that only forty-seven percent of construction laborers worked a full fifty or fifty-two weeks.

17

THE JOBS IN MACHINING

All-around Machinists

All-around machinists are highly skilled workers who use machine tools to make metal parts. They can set up and operate most types of machine tools. They are required to have a wide knowledge of shop operations and of the working properties of different metals, plus an understanding of what the different machine tools can do. This knowledge and skill enables them to turn a rough block of metal into an intricate part meeting precise specifications.

Variety is what makes the work of all-around machinists interesting and satisfying. They plan and carry through all operations needed in turning out machined products. They may switch frequently from the manufacture of one kind of product to another. They select the tools and material required for each job, and plan the cutting and finishing operations in order to complete the finished work according to blueprint or written specifications. They must, above all, have a good working knowledge of practical mathematics to make the shop computations relating to dimensions of work, tooling, feeds and speed of machines. They must also be able to use precision measuring instruments to check the accuracy of work. Then they may finish by hand, using files and scrapers, before assembling the finished parts with wrenches and screwdrivers.

The all-around machinist must also have a broad knowledge of the different types of metals. One of the jobs may be to heat-treat cutting tools and parts to improve their efficiency.

Many machinists are employed in maintenance departments to make or repair metal parts of machines and equipment. They must be able to test and adjust the parts they have made or repaired.

In plants that produce large numbers of metal products, some highly skilled machinists specialize in layout work. These **layout people** mark specifications on metal so that machine tool operators can perform the proper machining operations.

Almost every factory in the country using a large amount of machinery employs all-around machinists to keep its mechanical equipment operating. Some all-around machinists work in the production departments of metalworking factories where large quantities of identical parts are produced. Others work in machine shops where a limited number of varied products are made. Most of the all-around machinists work in these industries: machinery production, including electrical products; transportation equipment; fabricated metal products; metal-producing plants. Other industries where they are employed in substantial numbers are the railroad, chemical, food processing, and textile industries. The federal government employs them in Navy yards, Army arsenals, and other installations.

19

As industry becomes more mechanized, there is greater need for skilled machinists. In highly mechanized plants machine tools are often linked together by transfer equipment. In such plants, a breakdown of one machine may stop many other machines. The job of the machinist is to prevent such breakdowns, or if they should happen, to get the machinery working again—fast.

Working as a **machine tool operator** is often the first step toward becoming a more skilled machinist. Machine tool operators shape metal to precise dimensions by the use of machine tools. Most can operate only one or two types of machines; some can operate several. Many operators are unskilled workers who perform fairly simple, repeated operations that can be learned quickly. Other operators, more highly skilled, can perform complex and varied machining operations.

Machine Tool Operators

A typical job of a semi-skilled operator is to place rough metal stock in a machine tool on which the speeds and operation order have already been set by a skilled worker. This operator watches the machine and calls his supervisor if it is not functioning correctly. Special, easy-to-use gages help him to measure the work as it progresses. The operator who has limited training may make minor adjustments to keep his machine tool operating, but he depends on skilled machining workers for any major adjustments.

The more skilled machine tool operator usually

20

This operator is following an instruction sheet in setting up the tape controls for an external grinder.

(*Jones & Lamson photo*)

works with a single type of machine. The job involves little or no hand fitting or assembly work. On his machine, the operator plans and sets up the sequence of machine operations, working from blueprints, layouts, or other instructions. The proper tools must be selected for each operation. Then speed, feed, and other controls must be adjusted. The operator must also be familiar with all the special attachments for the machine. On completion of a job, the tolerances must be measured using micrometers, gages and other instruments. The skilled machine tool operator may also select and use cutting and lubricating oils to cool metal and tools during machining operations.

In the machining industry, these operators are

known by the kinds of machines they operate. For example, they are called **engine lathe operator, milling machine operator, drill press operator,** and so on.

Machine tool operators find work mainly in factories that manufacture fabricated metal products, transportation equipment, and machinery in large quantities. Skilled machine tool operators work in production departments, maintenance departments, and in toolrooms and job shops.

Instrument Makers

The growing use of instruments in production, research, development, and testing work is making the job of the **instrument makers** (also called experimental machinists and model makers) increasingly important. They work closely with engineers and scientists in translating designs and ideas into experimental models, special laboratory equipment, and custom instruments. They also modify existing instruments for special purposes.

Experimental devices constructed by these craftsmen are used, for example, to regulate heat, measure distance, record earthquakes, and control industrial processes. The mechanical instrument parts and models made by these workers range from simple gears to intricate parts of navigation systems for guided missiles and space vehicles.

Instrument makers fabricate metal parts by operating machine tools such as lathes and milling machines, and by using hand tools such as files

22

and chisels. Because accuracy is so important in their work, they measure finished parts with a variety of precision-measuring equipment, and special optical measuring devices.

Instrument makers work from rough sketches, verbal instructions, or ideas, as well as from detailed blueprints. In making parts they frequently have to use considerable imagination and ingenuity. Instrument makers sometimes work on parts that may not vary from specifications by more than ten millionths of an inch. To meet such standards they use many special electronic gages. They also work with a variety of materials, including plastics and rare metals such as titanium and rhodium.

An instrument maker may construct parts from start to finish, making and assembling all the parts and testing finished instruments for proper operation. However, in many large shops, or where electronic parts are used in making the instrument, they frequently work as one of a group, each making one or more parts of a complicated instrument.

Since they usually work on their own and have well-developed manual skills and reasoning ability, the instrument makers are a highly respected trade in the industry.

Many instrument makers are employed by firms which specialize in instrument making. Others work in research and development laboratories to make special devices used in scientific and medical research. Several thousand are employed by the federal government. Most of their jobs are centered around a few large cities, especially New York, Chicago, Los Angeles, Boston, Philadelphia, Washington, Detroit, Buffalo, Cleveland, and Rochester.

Machine Tool Job Setter

The **machine tool job setter,** usually called a setup man, although women are getting into this craft, is a skilled specialist employed in plant and machine shops that do machining work in large volume. Their main job is to set up machine tools; that is, to get machine tools ready for use by semi-

Tool setters have to "set up" the machine with the right cutting tools to do the job. On the table you can see the many different implements used by the setter.

(Jones & Lamson photo)

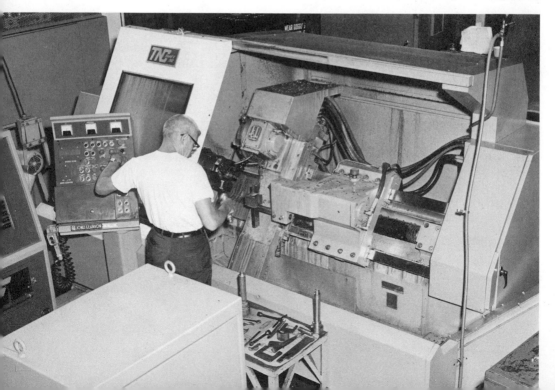

skilled operators. Then they explain to those workers the operations to be performed, and show them how to check the accuracy of their work.

Usually each setter is assigned a number of machine tools. Working from instructions, he or she sets up the machines with the proper cutting tools and decides on the rate at which the work will be fed into the machines.

Responsibilities of the job include adjusting the guides, stops and other controls, and setting the operation sequence—the order in which the machine performs its different functions. Then the setter may make trial runs and adjust the machine and tools until the parts produced meet specifications. Finally, the machine is turned over to a semi-skilled operator.

To get into setup work, you must usually qualify as an all-around machinist or skilled machine tool operator. The work requires thorough knowledge of one or more kinds of machine tools. It also calls for ability to read blueprints and make computations in selecting speeds and feeds for machine tools. The ability to communicate clearly is important, since the semi-skilled operators must be told how to perform the machining operations and how to check machining accuracy. Above all, this job calls for skill in selecting the sequence of operations so that metal parts will come out meeting specifications.

25

Most machinists doing setup work find their jobs in factories that manufacture metal products by mass production, make machinery, or produce transportation equipment. Practically all of their jobs are with companies that employ a large number of semi-skilled machine tool operators.

This boring machine is turning out a part for a large jet airplane engine.

(*Pratt & Whitney Aircraft photo*)

You may have seen a small, wood-cutting lathe in your school's machine shop. Look at the size of the work this machine is handling. The machinist must also know how to regulate the flow of coolant to keep the work from overheating.

(*Pratt & Whitney Aircraft photo*)

This operator is adjusting a milling machine. He works in a plant which produces the tool machines that go to factories throughout the United States and to foreign countries.

(*National Machine Tool Builders Association photo*)

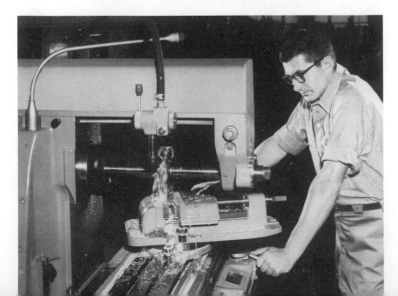

2/The Making of a Machinist

If this chapter were in a magazine, it would be called a "profile." It is the story of how one young man, Jack Franklin, became a career professional machinist in the tooling and machining industry.

Jack has always had a feeling for automobiles. Ever since he was old enough to get his driver's license during his sophomore year in high school,

Like many high school students, Jack Franklin ended his sophomore year with no idea of his future career.
(National Tool, Die & Precision Machining Association photo)

there has been a love affair between Jack and his car. He loved the styling of the smooth metal body and the feeling of power when the car moved. But most of all he liked the way the car *worked*—the way the engine turned, the drive of the axle.

Jack has been out of high school a few years now, but the same feelings are there every time he turns the key in the ignition.

There is also something that Jack feels about his car that others don't: a feeling of pride, and accomplishment. Today, you see, Jack Franklin is a **journeyman machinist.** And Jack Franklin happens to be one of the skilled craftsmen who helped manufacture one of the parts of the very car he owns!

A Feeling of Accomplishment

"It was during my third year of apprenticeship," Jack recalls. "I'd been working for a tool and die company ever since my pre-apprentice classes right after high school, when I was accepted for an on-the-job training program. I'd been given a lot of jobs and a lot of independent responsibility in those three years. Almost all the work was geared to a four-year syllabus of related skills education.

"I'd had the opportunity to work on lathes and grinders, jig-borers and special machines. But die making was what I liked best, and in my third year of apprenticeship I was able to spend most of my time working alongside older men who were experienced die makers."

Building a Bumper Die

That's when Jack helped build the die that eventually made the part on his new car.

"It was the front bumper," he recalls, "and it was one of the most fascinating experiences I've had. The work involved almost everything I'd learned during my three years on the job—from the basic shop math I'd learned in my first year to the highly advanced inspection methods I was taught when the die was in the try-out stage."

Jack and the men he worked with started out with a piece of steel weighing several tons. Their job was to cut and remove much of that metal to the close-tolerance specifications of their company's design engineers, often measured in thousandths of inches.

The end result of their work was a metal die used by one of the automotive companies to stamp out another piece of metal in the shape of Jack's bumper, and many thousands more just like it.

"I was darn proud of my work on that die," Jack says, "and a year or so later, when I saw that chromed bumper on the new car, I knew that was the automobile for me. How many other guys can own a car they helped build?"

How It Started —Looking for a Career

Now let's go back a few years. Like any number of his high school friends, Jack ended his sophomore year with little idea of the direction he wanted to take on a future career.

There were, however, some things he knew he

30

didn't want to do. Working behind a desk all day was one of them. "I'd always liked to do things with my hands," he says. "I was thinking along the lines of a career where I could apply whatever talents I had in that direction."

And Jack had already decided that a four-year spell of college wasn't for him. "I realized that it would have been a terrific strain on my family," he says, "and besides that, college just didn't appeal to me. I'd liked math and shop and a few other courses in high school—and I did pretty well —but the prospects of four more years of other subjects didn't really turn me on."

At the beginning of his junior year, Jack decided to sit down with his school's guidance counselor

From Jack's high school guidance counselor, he learned about the job of machinist and what it could offer him.
(*National Tool, Die & Precision Machining Association photo*)

to review his goals and possibly decide what direction to take. "That counseling opened up a lot of new ideas for me," Jack recalls. "My counselor told me about a lot of fields I never knew existed, the kinds of jobs and careers where I could apply my mechanical skills and look forward to an interesting and exciting future."

One of the fields Jack learned about from his counselor was the tooling and machining industry. His counseling sessions led him to decide to take as many vocational courses as he could for the remainder of his high school education. His family agreed that good vocational and shop courses would help prepare him for an eventual career where he could use his hands and mechanical abilities.

As Jack moved into his senior year, he began to investigate a career as a machinist more thoroughly. He says, "When I began to get into what I wanted to do, I found that becoming a machinist offered a lot of advantages for a guy like me."

Jack talked to his school counselor more frequently during that period. He also discussed his plans with his father and his friends. "I even talked with a couple of industry plant owners in our town," he says.

Listing Career Goals

Of course Jack had his own ideas about what he wanted, too. "I made a list," he remembers, "and put everything down in black and white. For

32

example, I put job security at the head of the list. That was important.

"I also knew I wanted good wages, and I wanted to make some money *now,* not after four years of college and then job hunting. I was also interested in being able to change jobs, or possibly work in a different part of the country after I'd gotten my feet wet in a career. I didn't plan to job-hop, but wanted to know whether I could move around if I had the opportunity."

And then there were the intangibles, which Jack remembers having had a hard time putting into words. As he explains, "It all boils down to the fact that I didn't want to be a cog on an assembly line somewhere. I wanted a personal identity. I wanted my own place and my own role in whatever I was doing.

"And, like everybody else, I guess I had the idea of someday perhaps making it on my own. Maybe owning my own business."

Jack applied these ideas—his list of qualifications, as he puts it—to a number of potential careers. He kept coming back to the idea of a career as a machinist.

Tops on Jack's list was **job security,** and a career as a machinist scored high. His counselor told him that there was almost always a demand for skilled machinists. In fact, there have never been enough to meet industry's needs. And today many

What a Machinist's Work Offers

of the country's machinists are men in their sixties, which means that young men entering the field have an open road ahead of them.

The earning potential for a skilled professional in the tooling and machining industry was excellent, Jack learned. His counselor provided him with some statistics published by the U. S. Department of Labor.

"Those figures were a real eye opener," Jack says. "I learned that the skilled tool makers and machinists enjoy a far higher lifetime income than most other workers, including those in the highly paid construction industry.

"And if you count the money a machinist makes during his four years of apprenticeship against the cost of going through four years of college, machinists earn a higher lifetime income than chemists, accountants, or pharmacists."

Earning Power **Earning power** was an important consideration for Jack. The fact that he would be earning while learning the machinist trade was an important factor in his decision. As he put it, "Even at a conservative estimate, I figured I'd have to spend about four thousand dollars a year for college expenses, plus more for living costs. At the bare minimum that's over sixteen thousand dollars over four years."

On the other hand, Jack discovered that he could count on making more than five thousand dollars during his first year as an apprentice, with about a one-thousand-dollar increase each year. After four years, that's an income of twenty-six thousand dollars.

Jack matched what we called his "intangible" list against a career as a machinist. With machinists usually in demand all over the country, he would have the **mobility** he sought.

Career Intangibles

What about his ideal of **personal identity,** and what he calls the "great American dream" of someday owning his own business?

As Jack put it, "One of the first things you find out about this business is that the skilled industry professional is an individual—a craftsman. He controls and sees the results of his work. He's not a human digit on a production line where machines master men. He masters the machine and uses it with the skill of an artist."

And as for owning his own business?

"That's where my talks with some of the plant owners came in handy," Jack recalls. "I found that the majority of the plants in the industry are owned by men who themselves started in shops as apprentices. Sure, there's no set formula for working into your own business—but the opportunity is there."

From the time he neared graduation from high school, the signals were all "go" for Jack Franklin to become a machinist. But then what?

35

**Becoming a
Machinist**

From his talks with his school guidance counselor, local people in this industry, and an adviser at the local office of the United States Employment Service, Jack knew there were a number of ways to start working toward his selected career.

Most of the men and women in the tooling and machine industry become apprentices with little formal training other than high school shop courses, previous work experience, or related work in the armed services. They move into their apprentice jobs directly after graduation or come into the industry from some other occupation.

This is the traditional method of beginning an apprenticeship, and most skilled employees in the country's shops started out that way.

But Jack also learned that there is another route for young men and women who want to become machinists. This is **pre-apprentice training,** which is available in many parts of the country.

Very simply, this is a system of providing a person interested in becoming a machinist-apprentice with specialized training prior to employment in an industry plant. This pre-apprentice training varies from area to area. In some parts of the country it takes the form of specialized classes in continuing education offered by state and municipal education offices. These often are conducted at local vocational schools or junior colleges.

In other areas pre-apprentice training may be

36

offered by local organizations made up of industry plants. Some correspondence schools offer similar courses.

Depending on the particular circumstances or the local situation, the courses may vary in terms of quality, length of study, and the investment in time and money a prospective apprentice may have to make.

Jack was fortunate enough to find in his town a pre-apprentice program conducted by the industry's national trade association, the National Tool, Die and Precision Machining Association. This program, more than ten years old, is run jointly by the Association and the federal government.

One of the first things Jack learned was that not everyone is accepted for this training. "You have to go through a couple of interviews and take aptitude tests," he reports. "That's when my vocational courses and mechanical drawing, math, and shop came in handy. I passed the test with flying colors."

Jack was entered in the next available pre-training class. Working on a five-day week, Jack and the other students divided shop work and classroom work each day, learning the fundamentals of the machinist's craft. At the end of the pre-training course (which varies from eight to sixteen weeks, depending on the locale) they were ready to start on their actual apprentice programs.

But first, they had to be hired as apprentices.

On-the-job Training

"The people at the training center were with us all the way," Jack says. "In addition to the instruction and counseling, they worked hard to assure that all of us had jobs by the end of the course. In my class, everyone was hired by local plants."

Jack had interviews with four different companies before settling on the one he is with now. The next four years went by quickly. The work was good—sometimes difficult, sometimes frustrating, but always interesting and different.

Moving Up

He started his new job at over two dollars an hour, and throughout the four years of his appren-

The pre-apprentice training classes got Jack off to a good start, but the competition was keen. He found that some girls in the class were out for the same jobs.

(*National Tool, Die & Precision Machining Association photo*)

Being off just the thickness of a human hair can mean a rejected job. Here, one of the experienced men helps Jack on a set-up measurement.

(National Tool, Die & Precision Machining Association photo)

ticeship that hourly rate was to rise as Jack progressed. Toward the end of his fourth year he was making as much as four dollars an hour with ample opportunity for overtime. During his apprenticeship, Jack was drawing a salary, learning, and contributing to his company's production.

The apprenticeship requirements are that you obtain a minimum of 2,000 hours of shop work annually and 144 hours of classroom study each year. Jack met that requirement by attending classes at a local training center once a week for thirty-six weeks out of the year.

After he completed his apprenticeship, Jack along with other new machinist journeymen re-

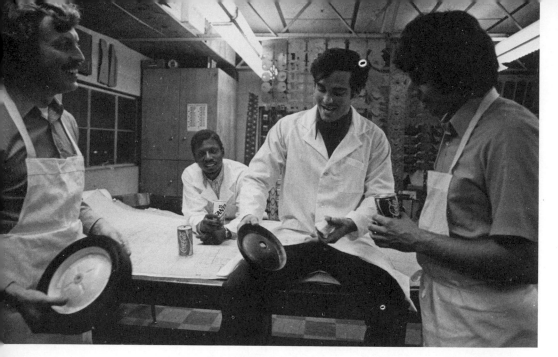

A bit of a celebration. Jack shows the end-product of a job he helped set up during his apprenticeship.

(National Tool, Die & Precision Machining Association photo)

ceived his certificate at a special dinner where a number of local tool and machining companies honored the graduates. Jack says, "I was darned proud when I stood up in front of my family and [by then he had married] my wife, and received that journeyman certificate."

The Work of the Journeyman

Now Jack Franklin is a **journeyman machinist**, recognized as a skilled professional wherever he goes, in whatever part of the country. He's still building dies, but now they are often a lot more complex than that front bumper die he built back in his third year on the job. But he still gets that feeling of pride when he looks at a completed die

40

on the tryout press, or the finished product that bears his craftsmanship.

"I can name dozens of major parts for cars and appliances that I've helped build dies for in the past couple of years. It's a nice feeling to know you've made a contribution like that, that someone is getting a lot of enjoyment or use out of a product which was built with your ingenuity and skill," he says.

"Unlike a lot of fellows I know," Jack adds, "I actually look forward to each day's work."

That work begins at seven a.m. each day at his plant. The company employs about thirty skilled workers, which they say is about average for the industry. Some companies may be as small as two- or three-man shops, others may employ as many as 250 to 300 machinists.

But there is more to a plant than workers and the building. There are the all-important machines and tools. The tools can range from a $2 screwdriver all the way up to a $350,000 die sinker. Some of the machines can remove a half inch of steel from a three-pound plate; others can grind one ten-thousandths of an inch from a four-ton cylinder. And there is a wide variety of metals for different operations, all of which require specialized handling.

And then there is a very broad range of instruments. Some are as simple as a six-inch rule.

41

Others are so exact that they can divide an inch into 100,000 parts . . . or more. Some instruments are so sensitive that if you push against a four-inch-square piece of metal twenty feet long, the instrument will measure the bend in the bar.

It Takes Skill   Let's take a look at what Jack and the other skilled workers in his plant do.

Their basic work is to **shape metals** and other materials to meet specifications within size limits usually measured in *thousandths of inches.*

Technically speaking, a true machinist makes precision parts. A die maker (or mold maker) like Jack performs the same basic work as other machinists, though using a slightly different approach. Jack's die will be used to make other parts. They must be machined as precisely as is humanly and engineeringly possible so that the parts made from them will be identical. It is upon this kind of precision work that most of American industry is based today.

"Put another way," adds Jack, "the machinist will make finished parts to **specific tolerances.** The mold and die maker makes molds and dies from which finished parts will be formed to equally close tolerance."

Tolerance means simply the leeway, or variance, the machinist is allowed. If he is shaping a piece of metal which calls for a length of three inches, his blueprint will usually require three inches plus

42

or minus .003 of an inch. So he must finish with a piece of metal that is within three thousandths of an inch of the three-inch specification.

"When you know that a human hair measures just about three thousandths of an inch in diameter," Jack notes, "you get a feel of how fine these tolerances are. And quite often, no tolerance at all is permitted."

It is not uncommon for a die maker like Jack to start with a piece of steel weighing as much as twelve tons. By the time he has removed the unneeded metal and cut or ground down to the desired specifications, he may end up with a finished assembly weighing only seven tons.

"This means I will have had to remove five tons of metal and end up with a product which may be within one ten-thousandth of an inch of specification," Jack says. "At the other extreme, a machinist may start with a piece of metal weighing only three pounds, and end up with a finished part weighing six ounces."

That is the goal of machinists, precision! If you think you would like to follow Jack Franklin's path to becoming a machinist, the following chapters in this book will show how *you* can be a machinist.

For More Information

3 / The Apprentice Program

In the last chapter you saw how Jack Franklin acquired the skills of a machinist in a four-year **apprentice program.**

How to Get Started

If you feel that machinist work appeals to you, how do you get started?

Most important, you should plan to complete high school. It is almost impossible to become a machinist without the right high school training. In Chapter Five you will find out how to take advantage of your high school courses to prepare for a career as a machinist. Some ambitious workers have managed to become machinists without high school training, by taking correspondence-school courses or enrolling in courses at trade or vocational schools after working hours, but that is a hard route to a career as a machinist.

The Apprentice System

The usual way to enter the machinist's trade is through a formal four-year apprenticeship. Apprenticeship is a work-study program under a written, formal agreement between the apprentice and the organization that conducts the program. That organization may be a chapter of a machinists' union, an employer or group of employers, or a

Learning to read and follow the instructions on blueprints is one of the most important parts of training for a machinist's job.

(Pratt & Whitney Aircraft photo)

trade association. The apprenticeship programs are conducted under the supervision of state or federal government agencies.

A typical apprentice program describes its admission requirements as the following:

Admission Requirements

"**Apprentice-trainees** will be selected through personal interview and aptitude testing regardless of race, color, age, religion, sex or national origin. Selection will be based in part on scholastic standing, personality, motivation, ambition, willingness to accept directions, mechanical ability and phys-

45

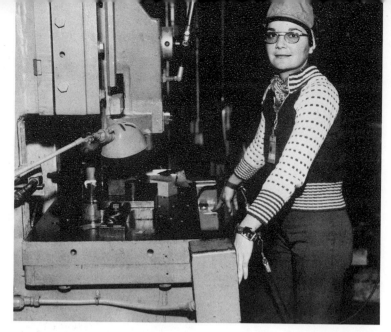

In recent years, more and more women have entered the machinist's world. This machinist is operating a mechanical press. Notice the protective devices to keep her hands away when the press descends.

(*Pratt & Whitney Aircraft photo*)

ical condition. Only those applicants who meet the following basic requirements will be considered:

"1. The applicant must be at least 18 years of age, and

"2. Must be a high school graduate or possess equivalent education, and

"3. Must have satisfactorily completed one year of algebra or geometry, or equivalent shop mathematics. Additional related mathematics and science subjects are preferred.

"4. Must pass the required physical examination."

The Apprentice Program

Many employers encourage workers to apply for the training offered in their company's apprentice programs. For example, the large Pratt & Whitney Aircraft Corporation in Connecticut sent this notice to its supervisors:

"It is to the advantage of the Company, to you, and to your people to provide all your employees with as much training and education as possible. You are also reminded of the Company's Affirmative Action Program and of your obligation to encourage minority and female members of your work force to apply for training opportunities. If they do not have the minimum requirements to enter a particular course, you should encourage them to obtain the necessary qualifications through the Company's Educational Assistance Program."

Probationary Period

In some programs apprentice-trainees are considered to be on probation during the first six months of their apprenticeship; in others the probationary period may extend throughout the whole training program. On graduation they are subject to the same rules and regulations governing other hourly or salaried employees and as stipulated by the union contract, if the company has a union agreement.

Tools

In many apprentice programs, apprentices within the first six months of training will be supplied with a set of tools which they pay for through weekly payroll deductions. On graduation, some

47

companies give the apprentice a cash bonus, sometimes $100 to partly defray the cost of the tools they were required to purchase.

Progress Reports

The work of each apprentice is checked at about three-month periods and the results are discussed with the apprentice privately by the **apprentice supervisor.** A copy of the progress report will be sent to parent or guardian on request.

Rate of Pay

The starting pay rate of the apprentice may vary in different parts of the country and in different companies, depending on the rate paid to the skilled machinists. Generally the apprentice begins at about half of the skilled machinist's pay rate and advances to about eighty percent of that rate by the time he or she completes the apprenticeship training.

Ralph E. Flanders of Vermont, who became a distinguished U.S. Senator, began his working life as a machinist apprentice in 1897. He worked 10 hours a day and received 4 cents an hour in the first year, and a few cents more during the second and third years of his apprenticeship. His annual wage in his last year of training was $295. He has described his apprenticeship as an old-fashioned one because he was legally indentured. His father was required to post a cash bond to be forfeited if the training was not completed. Young Flanders successfully finished his training, however, and later received degrees from various universities. He had an extensive industrial career before entering public life.

(*Courtesy U. S. Department of Labor*)

TERMS OF APPRENTICESHIP

TO THE

Brown & Sharpe Manufacturing Company,

PROVIDENCE, R. I.

Manufacturers of Fine Machinery and Machine Tools, &c.

This Agreement, made and entered into this _14th_ day of _January_ A. D. 18_77_, by and between the BROWN & SHARPE MANUFACTURING COMPANY, a corporation duly incorporated and located and doing business in the City of Providence, of the first part _Ralph E Flanders_ of _Lincoln, R. I._ of the second part, and _Albert W Flanders_ of _Lincoln R. I._ of the third part.

Witnesseth, That whereas the party of the second part is desirous of becoming an apprentice to said party of the first part, for the purpose of acquiring the art or trade of machinist, the said party of the first part, in consideration of the sum of One Hundred Dollars to it paid by said party of the third part, hereby accepts said party of the second part as an apprentice in the art or trade of machinist, in accordance with and subject to the "Terms of Apprenticeship" hereto annexed and made a part hereof.

And the party of the second part, in consideration of such acceptance, hereby agrees to become the apprentice of said party of the first part in the machinists' art or trade, in accordance with the "Terms of Apprenticeship" hereto annexed, and to faithfully conform with the provisions thereof.

And the party of the third part, in consideration of the execution of this agreement by said party of the first part, for himself, his heirs, executors and administrators, covenants and agrees to and with said party of the first part, that the party of the second part shall well and truly conform to and abide by all the provisions of said "Terms of Apprenticeship," and in case said party of the second part shall in any wise violate any of the provisions thereof, or shall abandon such apprenticeship before the expiration thereof, without the consent of said party of the first part, to pay to said party of the first part the sum of One Hundred Dollars as ascertained and liquidated damages for such breach of contract.

And the parties of the second and third parts respectively, for the considerations above set forth, also hereby covenant and agree to and with said party of the first part, that in the event that said apprentice shall be discharged for unfaithfulness, non-conformity with the rules and regulations which are or may be adopted for the good government of the shop, want of diligence, indifference to his business, or improper conduct in or out of the shop, or shall abandon such apprenticeship before the expiration thereof, without the consent of said party of the first part, all wages then earned by said party of the second part, and unpaid, shall be forfeited.

And the party of the first part further convenants and agrees, that in the event that said party of the second part shall remain its apprentice during the full term of apprenticeship (including the making up of lost time), as provided in the annexed "Terms of Apprentice-ship," and shall in all respects comply with the provisions of said "Terms of Apprenticeship," and shall not be discharged by reason of non-compliance therewith, to pay to said party of the third part, in consideration of such faithful service on the part of said apprentice, the sum of One Hundred Dollars.

In Witness Whereof, the parties aforesaid have hereunto set their hands and seals (the party of the first part by _Lucian Sharpe_ its _Treasurer_ duly authorized for that purpose,) the day and year first above written.

Executed } in presence of

Brown & Sharpe Mfg Co.

L. Sharpe Treas.

George Hunter Jr.   _Ralph E F Flanders_

Albert W Flanders

This is to certify that Ralph E Flanders has served his full term of apprenticeship according to the above agreement Feb 8. 1900 Brown & Sharpe Mfg Co. R. Viall, Supt.

APPRENTICE INDENTURE OF RALPH E. FLANDERS

Here is a modern apprentice pay scale, showing the increases in the past few years:

	Effective 12/04/72	Effective 12/03/73	Effective 1/6/75
Starting Rate	$3.25	$3.43	$3.94
1000 Hours	3.40	3.59	4.12
2000 Hours	3.56	3.76	4.31
3000 Hours	3.72	3.93	4.51
4000 Hours	3.89	4.10	4.71
5000 Hours	4.06	4.28	4.91
6000 Hours*	4.25	4.48	5.13
7000 Hours	4.44	4.68	5.38
8000 Hours**	4.64	4.90	5.66

*   6000 Hours graduation rate.

**   8000 Hours graduation rate.

What You Will Learn

The apprentice program is carefully planned to prepare you to handle the work of the machinist. On the next few pages you will see what the apprentice learns in the shop, sometimes called "hands-on" instruction, and in the classroom, called "related" instruction.

This is the six-thousand-hour machinist apprenticeship schedule of shop work:

50

	Approx. Hrs.
Machines	
Lathes	1045
Engine	
Turret	
Vertical Turret	
Automatic	
Right Angle	
Millers	830
Horizontal	
Vertical	
Universal	
Hydrotel	
Grinders	500
Internal	
External	
Surface	
Cutter	
Thread	
Gear Machines	200
Shaper	
Cutter	
Grinder	
Drills	200
Sensitive	
Radial	
Barnes	
Boring Mills & Jig Mills	400
Numerical Controlled Machines	280
Bench Assignment	600
Burring, Lapping, Fitting	
Assembly & Layout	
Inspection	310
Advanced Machining Methods	320
Heat Treating & Plating	160
Sheet Metal Familiarization	80
Welding Familiarization	40
Presses	80
Tool Cribs	80
Plastics & Model Making	40
Classroom Work	835
TOTAL HOURS	6000

SIX THOUSAND HOUR
MACHINIST APPRENTICESHIP
SCHEDULE OF CLASSROOM WORK

	Approx. Hrs.
Mathematics	185
Arithmetic	
Algebra	
Geometry	
Geometric Construction	
Trigonometry	
Blueprint Reading	125
Orthographic & Isometric Projection	
Lines, Notes & Symbols	
Auxiliary & Section Views	
Machine Part & Sheet Metal Prints	
Tool, Die & Gage Prints	
Pattern Drafting	
Assembly Prints	
Practical Descriptive Geometry	50
Theory	
Graphic Problems	
True Lengths & Proportions	
Primary & Secondary Auxiliary Views	
Theory	50
Machine Theory	
Geor Theory	
Metallurgy & Industrial Processes	40
Sources, Identification, Properties	
& Uses of Metals	
Working Properties of Metals	
Methods of Manufacturing Aircraft	
Engine Parts	
Economics	15
Business Organization	
Economic Growth	
English	20
Trade Literature	
Shop Orders & Records	
Report Writing	

52

The Apprentice Program

Job Instruction Training	20
Practical Shop & Mechanical Problems	80
Application of practical classroom	
material, including Scale Layout,	
Template Drafting and Design Theory,	
to current shop problems.	
Applied Physics	40
Mechanics	
Non Destructive Testing	
Measuring Tools	15
Reading, Care & Application	
Machinery's Handbook	15
Reference Procedures	
Problem Solving	
Numerical Control Familiarization	20
Machine Theory	
Programming Theory	
Orientation	50
Company Familiarization	
Product Familiarization	
Personal Development	80
Human Relations, Leadership & Cases	
Oral Communications	
Discussion Leading & Listening	
Methods of Instruction	
Safety	30
TOTAL CLASSROOM HOURS	835

EIGHT THOUSAND HOUR
TOOLMAKER & DIEMAKER
APPRENTICESHIP SCHEDULES OF
SHOP AND CLASSROOM WORK

Graduates of the 6000 Hour Machinist Apprenticeship Course will be eligible for consideration for an additional 2000 hours training as Toolmakers or Diemakers. Considered, will be those with definite interests and aptitudes for this work who are in the upper half of their group.

53

	Approx. Hrs.
Related Training	200
Mechanics	
Mechanisms	
Tool Design	
Die Design	
Jig & Fixture Design	
Metallurgy	
Shop Training	1800
Jig Bore & Boring Mill	
Profiling & Contour Work	
Bench Work	
Jig & Fixture Repair	
New Dies	
Die Repair	
Die Sharpening	
Heat Treat	
Plastic Tooling	
TOTAL HOURS	2000

For More Information

If you are seriously interested in becoming an apprentice machinist, you have to show some initiative. The job won't come to you.

The Bureau of Apprenticeship and Training Field Offices and the State Apprenticeship Agencies listed in the appendixes at the back of this book may be able to provide you with information on apprentice opportunities in your area.

The National Machine Tool Builders Association, 2139 Wisconsin Ave. N.W., Washington, D.C., offers information on apprentice training, especially for tool and die makers.

Many state employment offices, which you will find listed under the name of your state in the telephone book, provide free aptitude testing to persons interested in becoming all-around machinists or tool and die makers. The state employment service may also be a source of information about training opportunities under the Manpower Development and Training Act. In addition, the state employment service refers applicants for apprentice programs to employers.

This Certificate of Completion can be worth much more to you than a college diploma. It is awarded by the apprenticeship agency in your state, or by the Federal Committee on Apprenticeship if your state has no such agency. It is recognized everywhere as proof that you have become a skilled craftsman, and can lead to a lifetime of highly paid employment in your chosen trade.

Apprenticeship information may also be obtained from the following unions (which have local offices in many cities):

International Association of Machinists and Aerospace Workers, 1300 Connecticut Avenue. N.W., Washington, D.C. 20036

International Union, United Automobile, Aerospace and Agricultural Implement Workers of America, 8000 East Jefferson Ave., Detroit, Michigan 48214.

International Union of Electrical, Radio and Machine Workers, 1126 16th St. N.W., Washington, D.C. 20036.

This trainee is setting up a Gleason Gear Grinder.
(*Pratt & Whitney Aircraft photo*)

4 / Other Ways to Enter the Trade

In the last chapter you saw how apprentice programs can lead to a career in the machinists' trades. Now we will take a look at some other ways to get into this work. Perhaps one of these suggestions will be your answer to the problem of becoming a machinist.

The **Job Corps** is a government training program for young people sixteen to twenty-one years of age who have dropped out of school and can't find a job. Youths from all races, religions, and national origins are eligible for this program.

The Job Corps

The basic purpose of the Job Corps training centers is to give these young people training that will improve their chances of getting a good job with future possibilities of security and advancement. The classroom training is designed to help you make up what you missed in school. For example, if your goal is a machinist's job, the center will help you work toward a high school or equivalency diploma, with the necessary mathematics and science courses. The work program at the Center will give you a chance to develop good work habits.

An underseas machinist! This U. S. Navy machinist mate is operating a lathe in the machinery space aboard a nuclear-powered ballistic missile submarine.

As a corpsman (girls are eligible for this program, too), you will live at one of the centers which are located in various parts of the country. Some are in national parks or in forests; others are in or near large cities.

Although the Job Corps tries to find jobs for its graduates in their desired fields, some graduates prefer to return to school, and others enter the armed forces.

Job Corps Benefits

At the centers, the corpsmen get comfortable living quarters and free medical and dental care, clothes and other necessities. In return, they are expected to attend classes regularly and do their share in the work program. They must care for their own rooms and clothing, and do chores to keep the center in order. They are expected to follow the Job Corps behavior rules and regulations. A corpsman may be sent home if he or she breaks the rules.

Enrollees are given a spending allowance of thirty dollars a month. When they finish their training—which may be for one or two years— they receive what is called a "readjustment allowance": fifty dollars for each month of satisfactory service in the Job Corps. Under a special agreement, if the corpsman wants to send money home to his family he can send them up to twenty-five dollars each month he is in the Corps. The Job Corps will match the amount sent. For example, if the corpsman wants to send twenty-five dollars to his family each month, the Corps will match that and the family will receive fifty dollars.

After six months of satisfactory service corpsmen are eligible for home leave once a year, with round-trip transportation paid by the government.

Some Job Corps enrollees have problems. Some find it hard to adjust to life at the center, because it is very different from living at home. There is a certain amount of discipline; a fairly rigid timetable must be followed; living with a large group of other young people may create conflicts.

If you apply for the Jobs Corps when you are still a minor, you must have the written consent of your parent or guardian.

For More
Information

To find out more about the Job Corps, you can visit or write your nearest state employment service, or write to this address:

> U. S. Department of Labor
> Manpower Administration
> Job Corps
> Washington, D.C. 20210

Working
for the
Government

Earlier in this book, you found that the federal government employs thousands of machinists in arsenals, Navy yards, repair shops and other installations. Many of these are already skilled machinists who apply for government jobs which offer good job security, civil service benefits such as health and medical programs, vacations, retirement provisions, and rates of pay that meet those of private industry.

But many of the machinists employed by the government have been trained by the government while being paid, very much as in the apprentice program in private industry.

How do you go about getting a government machinist-trainee job?

The first step is to file your application with the U. S. Government Civil Service Commission, the agency which is in charge of filling government jobs. You will find a list of offices in Appendix B (page 110).

Other Ways to Enter the Trade

You can call or write to the office covering the place where you live. Ask for an application for machinist-trainee. In reply, you will receive an application form to be filled out and returned. Then, when there are openings, you will be notified.

But just asking for the job does not mean that you will be hired. There is much competition for the jobs. You will be called in for a personal interview and will be given an aptitude test and a physical examination. If you are hired, you will be on probation for the first months to find out how you are working out on the job.

A typical government program is the one at the Rock Island, Illinois, arsenal. It is known as the

A machine tool operator trainee at a U. S. arsenal loads a part to be drilled. Like many others, he came into the arsenal through a veterans' readjustment program and is receiving training in all phases of machinist's work.

(*U. S. Army photo*)

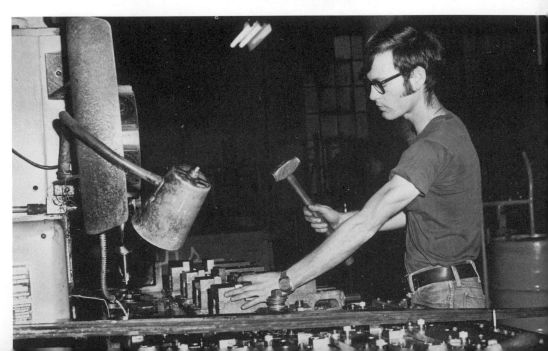

A Government
Training
Program

"Helper/Intermediate Training Program" to develop proficient machinists and tradesmen at the arsenal. During the last three years more than 371 persons were hired under that program.

The training program consists of both on-the-job training and classroom instruction, which is conducted at the arsenal by instructors from a nearby college, Black Hawk College.

The arsenal says that "because of the shortage of qualified tradesmen in the area, filling machinist, tool operator and metal working positions has been difficult in the past. With the initiation of this program, however, employees are being trained to operate numerous machines and will be able to fill these positions."

Another problem at the arsenal has been the high retirement rate. Their personnel office says that 60 percent of the current machine tool operators are eligible to retire. This means that the training program will provide young trainees who can progress to higher grade levels as they become more skilled in their trade.

The training program is divided into two phases: Phase I covers a one-year period of training at $5.10 an hour; Phase II covers another year at $5.52 an hour. On completing the program the trainee is eligible for promotion to $5.72 an hour.

Classroom training during the two-year period covers fundamentals of shop math, blueprint reading, use of measuring instruments, basic layout procedures, and general math.

During the trainee's first year he spends about 120 hours in the classroom, and in his second year about 108 hours.

Trainees perform various kinds of work such as installing machinery units and parts, setting up heavy equipment, and operating machines such as turret lathes and drill presses.

In a recent class of 48, there were 13 women, five minority members, and 15 veterans; ages ranged from 18 to 55.

No specific amount of training or experience is required to apply for the program.

In addition to the federal government, many states and local governments hire both machinist-

State and Local Government

A new employee receives instruction in the operation of a Sundstrand Numerical Control Machining Center at the Puget Sound Naval Shipyard.

(*Machinist Magazine photo*)

trainees and skilled machinists. Your local state employment service office usually has information on such openings. You could also apply directly to the state Civil Service Commission, sometimes called Department of Personnel, at your state capital. Also, such job openings are often posted in your local post office building. In most states there are civil service newspapers that carry announcements of job openings and directions on how and where to apply for them.

Opportunities in the Armed Forces

If you are machinist-minded, you can learn this trade by enlistment in the armed services. As a volunteer, you can enlist with a written agreement that you will be trained for the trade you desire if you meet the qualifications.

The Navy uses more machinists than the other services, but there are opportunities in the Army.

In the Navy, **machinist mate** is the rating given to enlisted personnel doing this kind of work. The Navy points out that following naval training, you could be qualified as a civilian engine lathe operator, machinist, turret lathe operator, bench machinist, tool maker, milling machine operator, tool and die maker, or shaper operator.

The qualifications that the Navy asks are mechanical aptitude and a good head for figures. Also helpful but not essential are courses or experience in mathematics, machine shop, electricity, foundry work, mechanical drawing, and blueprint reading.

Other Ways to Enter the Trade

Following the basic recruit training, your preparation for the job would include on-the-job instruction, with individual study of naval manuals or service school courses in hand tool skills, shop mathematics, mechanical drawing and blueprint reading, identification and characteristics of metals, heat treatment, and machine tool operation.

Navy Training

Navy machinery repairmen work in Navy machine shops aboard ships and at repair bases and other shore stations.

If you think you would be interested in combining a military career with a career as a machinist, check with the nearest Army, Navy or Air Force recruiting office. You can find the address in the white pages of your local telephone directory under the heading "United States Government."

For More Information

65

5/High School and College Preparation

Math and Other Courses

If there is any one idea that this book should convey, it is the importance of mathematics to the machinist.

You can get a head start toward a career as a machinist by taking every mathematics course offered in your high school. Algebra, geometry, trigonometry, and any other mathematics course your high school offers will prove worthwhile to you in getting a job as a machinist, and succeeding in the field. If your school offers a course in metrics, be sure to apply for it. There are courses in the sciences, too, that you should take. Physics and chemistry have important applications in the world of the machinist. If your school has a machine shop, that will give you an idea of the work of the machinist, and the shop math usually given with shop work is also valuable.

There are other courses that may seem outside the machinist's requirements that can help you, too. In many machinists' jobs, the machinist has to prepare written instructions for other workers, or for the people who prepare the programmed tapes for numerical control machines. Taking ex-

66

tra courses in written English can help in that area.

A course in public speaking can be an asset to you. In many shops the skilled machinist has to show less skilled operators how to operate their machines, and a course that improves what teachers call "verbal communications" can be important.

In recent years many community colleges have been giving two-year courses that will grant you an associate degree in the field of machine work. In addition, there are private and public vocational schools that offers machinist training.

College Training

You can find out about such schools near you by writing to the Division of Vocational Training, State Department of Education, at your state cap-

These students are learning NC (numerical control) operations at Pierce College in Los Angeles. The first step is preparation of the tape which provides programmed instruction to the machines. Then the tape is tested on a computer.

(Pierce College photo)

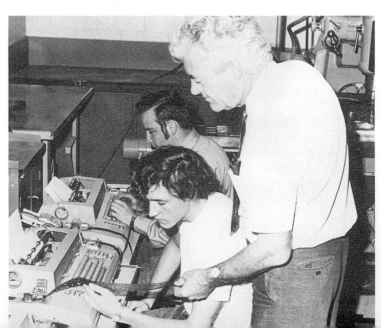

ital, asking for a list of accredited schools offering machinist training.

Many students who started such two-year courses have become interested in further education and have gone on to four-year colleges to obtain their degree in industrial engineering or other engineering fields.

The requirement for admission to these courses is a high school equivalency certificate. Many community colleges are free to residents of the state, while charging tuition fees to non-residents. Others charge residents a small fee, and non-residents higher tuition.

When you find a school whose courses interest you, write to the school for their catalog which will give you all the necessary information.

Here a group of students at Pierce College test a tape which has been prepared as part of their training in numerical control operations. (*Pierce College photo*)

6/The Aptitude Test

In many parts of the country, especially in larger cities, when you apply for a trainee-apprentice position with a large company or with a government agency, you may be asked to take a written examination known as an **aptitude test.** The purpose of such a test is not to find out how much you know about the trade but to find out whether you have the kind of mind to become a good trainee. In addition, the test may also require you to work with your hands to find out whether you have good **manual dexterity**—the ability to handle tools or work with objects. People who do this well have good **spatial imagery.** This is the ability to see how different objects fit together.

You can't really study for aptitude tests. But you can get ready to do your best on them by taking tests of different kinds that you can find in newspapers, magazines, quiz books, or in school-

How to Take Aptitude Tests

Not all aptitude tests are paper and pencil tests. On some you work with your hands.

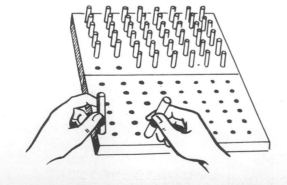

books. Be sure to set a time limit for yourself if one is not set for you. Any test you practice on can help you learn how to take tests. You will learn how questions are asked on tests and how to go about answering them.

What if you get nervous about taking tests? Some people complain that they get nervous when they take tests. Remember, everyone gets a little nervous when something important happens to him. In the same way that a pitcher warms up before a ball game, your mind and body are trying to warm up for the test by getting nervous.

If you are ready to take a test, you will be like a well-trained ballplayer. When you take a test, your nervousness will keep you alert but not tired out.

Give yourself extra time to get to the test and even be early so that you can sit down and relax for a few minutes before the test.

The people giving the test are there to help you. When you take a test, remember that the persons giving the test are not there to give you a rough time. They are there to help you know what to do on the test and how to go about it. If there is anything you do not understand, ask questions. Don't be the strong silent type who won't ask questions and then gets easy test questions wrong because he had the wrong idea about what he was supposed to do. Ask questions!

The Aptitude Test

Rule 1. *Work quickly.* Most aptitude tests have short time limits and a lot of questions. To get your best score, you must work quickly. If you stop and daydream during a test, or check each answer many times, you will not do as well as you could. Usually each test is made so long that you are not expected to finish it, but the more you do correctly, the better your score will be.

If you waste a lot of time on a hard question by trying to puzzle out the right answer or by changing the answer many times, you won't get to questions that might be easier. Don't let questions that you can't answer keep you from going on to questions that you may find easier. However, it is just as important to get the answers right as it is to do a lot of them. Don't try to go so fast that you give wrong answers to easy questions.

Rule 2. *If you think you know the right answer, put it down.* Don't be afraid to answer if you aren't sure you are right, but don't guess wildly.

Rule 3. *Always follow instructions.* Start work on the test when you are told to start, but not before. Stop when you are told to stop. A low score on a test may mean that you just didn't follow directions.

Rule 4. *Don't give up.* Don't be discouraged just because a test has a lot of hard questions. Some tests are easy, some hard. Remember that a hard test is hard for everyone who is taking it.

71

If you are worried that the entrance or aptitude test may stand between you and your chances of becoming a machinist, you can get help in preparing for the test. This kind of assistance is offered in most big cities, and in many smaller communities, through such organizations as the local AFL-CIO Building and Construction Trades Council, the Urban League, Workers Defense League, or other Community Action Agency. Another way to get help is to check with the local Apprenticeship Information Center of the U. S. Department of Labor. They will be able to give you information about attending one of the special four-week courses which are conducted to prepare applicants for apprenticeship tests as openings for jobs as apprentices become available in your area. You can find a listing of these offices on pages 104 to 109 in this book.

Directions for Taking Tests

When you go in to take the aptitude test, you will be seated at a desk or table and will be given a test booklet. On the front cover of the booklet you find "Directions" for taking the test. Do not open the booklet and start answering until you are told to do so.

Following are three "Directions" from commonly used aptitude tests for machinist-trainees or apprentices. Read them carefully and you will get a good idea of what to expect when you take your test.

DIRECTIONS

Fill in the requested information on your ANSWER SHEET.

Look at Sample X on this page. It shows two men carrying a weighted object on a plank, and it asks, "Which man carries more weight?" Because the object is closer to man "B" than to man "A," man "B" is shouldering more weight; so blacken the circle under "B" on your answer sheet. Now look at Sample Y and answer it yourself. Fill in the circle under the correct answer on your answer sheet.

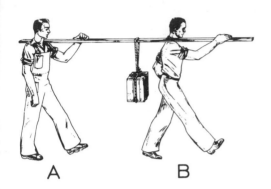

X

Which man carries more weight?
(If equal, mark **C**.)

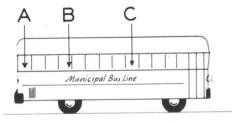

Y

Which letter shows the seat where a passenger will get the smoothest ride?

On the following pages there are more pictures and questions. Read each question carefully, look at the picture, and fill in the circle under the best answer on the answer sheet. Make sure that your marks are heavy and black. Erase completely any answer you wish to change. Do not make any marks in this booklet.

TEST OF MECHANICAL COMPREHENSION
FORM AA
George K. Bennett, Ph.D.

DIRECTIONS

Fill in the requested information on your ANSWER SHEET.

Now line up your answer sheet with the test booklet so that the "Page 1" arrow on the booklet meets the "Page 1" arrow on the answer sheet. Then look at Sample X on this page. It shows pictures of two rooms and asks, "Which room has more of an echo?" Because it has neither rugs nor curtains, there is more of an echo in room "A"; so blacken the space under "A" on your answer sheet. Now look at Sample Y and answer it yourself. Fill in the space under the correct answer on your answer sheet.

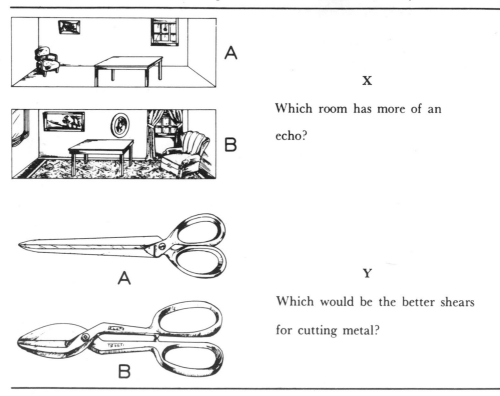

X

Which room has more of an echo?

Y

Which would be the better shears for cutting metal?

On the following pages there are more pictures and questions. Read each question carefully, look at the picture, and fill in the space under the best answer on the answer sheet. Make sure that your marks are heavy and black. Erase completely any answer you wish to change. Be certain that you use the right column on the answer sheet for each page. The arrow on the page should meet the arrow on the answer sheet.

DO NOT MARK THIS BOOKLET—PUT YOUR ANSWERS ON THE ANSWER SHEET.

DIRECTIONS AND PRACTICE PROBLEMS

READ THE FOLLOWING DIRECTIONS VERY CAREFULLY WHILE THE EXAMINER READS THEM ALOUD

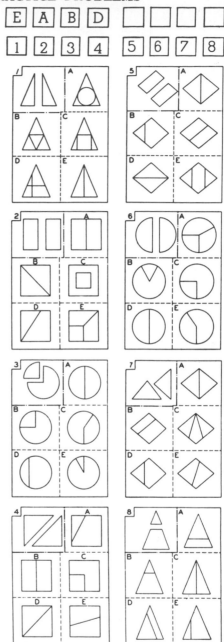

Look at the problems on the right side of this page. You will notice that there are eight of them, numbered from 1 to 8. Notice that the problems go DOWN the page.

First look at Problem 1. There are two parts in the upper left-hand corner. Now look at the five figures labelled A, B, C, D, E. You are to decide which figure shows how these parts can fit together. Let us first look at Figure A. You will notice that Figure A does **not** look like the parts in the upper left-hand would look when fitted together. Neither do Figures B, C, or D. Figure E **does** look like the parts in the upper left-hand corner would look when fitted together, so E is PRINTED in the square above ☐1 at the top of the page.

Now look at Problem 2. Decide which figure is the correct answer. As you will notice, Figure A is the correct answer, so A is printed in the square above ☐2 at the top of the page.

The answer to Problem 3 is B, so B is printed in the square above ☐3 at the top of the page.

In Problem 4, D is the correct answer, so D is printed in the square above ☐4 at the top of the page.

Now do Problems 5, 6, 7, and 8.

PRINT the letter of the correct answer in the square above the number of the example at the top of the page.

DO THESE PROBLEMS NOW.

If your answers are not the same as those which the examiner reads to you, RAISE YOUR HAND.

DO NOT OPEN THE BOOKLET UNTIL YOU ARE TOLD TO DO SO.

Some of the problems on the inside of this booklet are more difficult than those which you have already done, but the idea is exactly the same. In each problem you are to decide which figure shows the parts correctly fitted together. **Sometimes the parts have to be turned around, and sometimes they have to be turned over in order to make them fit.** In the square above ☐1 write the correct answer to Problem 1; in the square above ☐2 write the correct answer to Problem 2, and so on with the rest of the test. Start with Problem 1, and go DOWN the page. After you have finished one column, go right on with the next. **Be careful not to go so fast that you make mistakes.** Do not spend too much time on any one problem.

PRINT WITH CAPITAL LETTERS ONLY.

MAKE THEM SO THAT ANYONE CAN READ THEM.

DO NOT OPEN THE BOOKLET BEFORE YOU ARE TOLD TO DO SO.

YOU WILL HAVE EXACTLY 20 MINUTES TO DO THE WHOLE TEST.

7/Opportunities for Women

You Can Start Now

If you are a girl, and are interested in machine work as your future career, you can begin to prepare yourself now.

If your school offers courses in machine shop, machine shop mathematics, or other subjects geared to the machine trades, you have every right to sign up for them and to be accepted. The old idea of putting girls in domestic science classes and only the boys in trades classes has been outlawed by federal laws and by laws in almost every state. The same laws also provide that if boys want to take up cooking or sewing, they have every right to do so.

The apprenticeship programs and other programs described in this book are open to young women on an equal basis. As the situation is now, a girl will have a harder time making it than a man with equal qualifications, but it can be done.

Help for Women

In many parts of the country, special programs have been set up just to help women get into apprenticeship training programs.

One of these is the "Women in Apprenticeship Program," a project of Advocates for Women, a San Francisco, California, organization. That group has a contract with the U. S. Department

76

She's a pioneer! Beverly Mayo was the first woman tool grinder and repairer at her shop in the Rock Island Arsenal.

(*U. S. Army photo*)

of Labor, giving it the responsibility of placing women who have the basic qualifications into various apprenticeship training programs in the San Francisco Bay area.

Dorothea Hernandez, director of the Women in Apprenticeship Program, says that they have been successful in placing women in machinist positions in several large companies in their area.

In addition to machinist, they suggest other trade possibilities for which women should be qualified. This listing may interest you as a guide to other fields of employment:

The possibilities are: auto mechanic *, carpenter *, painter, welder, electrician *, plumber *, sheet metal worker, meatcutter, glazier, drywall worker, ironworker, roofer, bricklayer, plasterer, cement mason, tool and die maker, and heat and frost insulation installer.

There may be a program similar to the Advo-

* For those occupations marked with (*), there are books similar to this one in the *Vocations in Trades* series by this publisher.

Machine operator

American Machinist Magazine sent a photographer out to get pictures of women working as machinists. Here are some of the pictures he came back with.

(American Machinist Magazine photos)

Drill press operator

Drafting room worker

cates for Women in your area. You can find out by writing to:

> Women's Bureau
> U. S. Department of Labor
> 14th Street & Constitution Ave. N.W.
> Washington, D.C. 20210

The U. S. Department of Labor also has a free publication, "Careers for Women in the 70's." You can get a copy by writing to the Office of Information, Department of Labor, at the above address.

If you would like to learn more about the Advocates for Women Program and how it works, you can write to:

> Advocates for Women
> 593 Market Street—Suite 500
> San Francisco, California 94105

If you follow the national women's magazines, you will find that they are beginning to give a lot of space to their readers who are interested in mechanical trades. Magazines such as *Ms., Seventeen, Glamour,* and others frequently run articles about women who have been successful in the skilled trades and about the expanding possibilities for women in this kind of work.

79

8/VICA and the National Skill Olympics

VICA—
Goals and
Membership

If you are now in high school, find out whether there is a VICA chapter in your school. If there is no VICA chapter in your high school, tell your guidance counselor or shop teacher that you would be interested in joining a chapter. This is a sort of high school fraternity that is part of the Vocational Industrial Clubs of America. It takes in both boys and girls who are interested in preparing for jobs in industry and in trades, and machinist is among the fields. The aim is to give students who want to work with their hands a club with others who have the same interests.

As VICA explains its program, the goals are to "provide activities, foster a respect for the dignity of work; promote high standards in trade ethics, workmanship, scholarship and safety, and develop patriotism by practicing democracy."

The organization, which was started in 1965, now has almost 180,000 members in over 2,000 clubs and 39 state associations. Clubs in the high schools are joined together to form the state association. In addition to giving you a chance to

Contestant in the National VICA Skill Olympics setting up a lathe as part of his competition in the Machine Shop event.
(Vocational Industrial Clubs of America photo)

join a group with the same interests that you have, VICA works with the schools to set up special vocational training programs.

As a VICA member, you receive newsletters and a national magazine devoted to trade vocations. Also, VICA has local and national competitions that give you an opportunity to get the same kind of recognition that other students get participating in school athletics or debating teams. For example, each year competitions are held to determine who is the best student carpenter, bricklayer, machinist, plumber, or electrician.

In addition to machinist work, VICA members in your club may be training for any of these occupations:

81

VICA Trade Vocations

Air-conditioning mechanic
Aircraft mechanic
Appliance repairman
Auto-body repairman
Auto mechanic
Bricklayer
Building maintenance man
Cabinetmaker
Carpenter
Cement mason
Commercial artist
Cook
Cosmetologist
Dental assistant
Diesel mechanic
Draftsman
Dressmaker
Dry cleaner
Electrician
Fireman
Fishery occupations
Food trade worker
Instrument repairman
Ironworker
Janitor
Jeweler and watchmaker
Laboratory assistant

Launderer
Maintenance mechanic
Meatcutter
Medical assistant
Nurse's aid
Optical mechanic
Painter
Paperhanger
Patternmaker
Photographer
Pipe fitter
Plasterer
Plumber
Practical nurse
Presser
Printer
Radio and television
    repairman
Sewing machine operator
Sheet-metal worker
Shipbuilding
Shoe repairman
Tailor
Textile worker
Tile setter
Tool and die maker
Welder

Instruction

Industry organizations work with the national VICA organization to help set up vocational training programs in the high schools. For instance, in a VICA-industry training program for machinist trainees, you would have three-hour classes in the school shop or on the job, five days a week, over a two-year period. In addition to the trade skill training, you would be taught related theory. In all, you would receive 1,000 hours of machinist or related instruction, and you would

82

be given credit for much of this time when you were accepted as a machinist apprentice.

To give you an idea of how the VICA U. S. Skill Olympics operates, here are the rules which apply to contestants from all over the country.

VICA U. S. Skill Olympics

VICA U. S. SKILL OLYMPICS
MACHINE SHOP CONTEST

PURPOSE
To promote trade excellence in a competitive situation and give machine shop students an opportunity to demonstrate the basic skills of their field.

CLOTHING REQUIREMENT
White trousers, white shirt, regular work shoes, safety glasses.

OBSERVER RULE
(1) A roped or marked area will be designated for observers. No observer, including VICA advisors, will be outside this area. (2) Observers shall not talk or gesture to contestants. (3) Judges will penalize contestants if they accept assistance from observers (observers should be warned before penalty occurs). (4) Observers will not be allowed in the assembly area.

PROCEDURE
1. Contestants will draw numbers for identification during the pre-contest orientation meeting.
2. Contestants will assemble at the contest site at the announced contest time for last-minute instructions. They will have the tools which are required in these rules.

RULES
1. One contestant per state from each division will be allowed to compete.
2. All materials and facilities will be provided by the contest chairman.
3. Contestants will be judged on ability to perform one or more machine operations similar to the types of operations listed below:
   a. *Sharpen a basic cutting tool and operate same*
   b. *Operate a lathe*
      Example—Indicate a 1″ piece of round stock in a 4-jaw chuck and reduce diameter to ¾″ with corresponding concentricity check.

Machine Shop Contest Rules

   c. *Operate a milling machine*

      Example—With a provided piece of mild steel and a vertical mill, machine a ½″ by ⅛″ slot 1.5000 from edge with a corresponding check for tolerance limits.

   d. *Surface grinder operation*

      Example—With a provided piece of heat-treated steel grind 3 sides square.

   e. *Precision measurements*

      Example—With given measuring devices, measure and record dimensions or using height gage, lay out given design, etc.

4. Contestant must supply safety glasses.
5. Contestant will receive stock blanks on which all operations will be performed.
6. Contestant will receive working drawing with specifications of jobs to be completed.
7. Judges will be present to observe proceedings of the entire contest.
8. Each contestant will draw an identifying number at the time of registration.

REQUIRED CONTEST PERSONNEL

1. Contest chairman
2. Five judges
3. Student guide
4. Timekeeper

INSTRUCTIONS TO CONTEST CHAIRMAN

1. The contest chairman will provide a judge for each of the operations required and as many timekeepers as necessary.
2. The contest chairman will assemble judges one-half hour before the contest to be certain all questions are answered and rating procedures are clear.
3. After judging is completed, judges will return rating sheets to contest chairman in envelope provided.
4. Job sheets and rating sheets will be provided by the contest chairman.
5. Supplies will be provided as specified.
6. Contestants will be allowed 15 minutes to become familiar with *all* machines to be used in the contest.

INSTRUCTIONS TO JUDGES

1. Careful consideration should be given to each rule and each entry should be judged exactly in the same manner and under the same conditions.

2. Judges should notice weights assigned to each area on the rating sheets.
3. Judges will meet at the contest site in advance of the contest, at an announced time, to confer on (a) rule meanings (b) room arrangements (c) materials and equipment and (d) the selection or election of a chairman of the judges.
4. Judges will know contestants by number only.
5. Judges will total their own rating sheets and return them to contest chairman in the envelope provided.
6. Judges will keep all information confidential until general announcement.

EQUIPMENT AND MATERIALS NEEDED
1. The technical committee will supply the tools, equipment and supplies as required for the skills selected.
2. Each contestant must supply the following tools:
   a. 1 each 0–1″ micrometer
   b. 1 each 1–2″ micrometer
   c. 6″ steel rule
   d. 1 each center gage
   e. 1 each 4″ or 6″ O.D. Spring caliper
   f. 1 each 4″ or 6″ I.D. Spring caliper
   g. $\frac{5}{16}$″ square turning tool
   h. $\frac{5}{16}$″ square facing tool
   i. $\frac{5}{16}$″ square threading tool
   j. $\frac{3}{16}$″ square boring tool for a half-inch Williams sleeve bar for boring internal shoulders

Awards and Information

The contest is part of the annual three-day meeting at which VICA members also compete for honors in club business procedure, displays, extemporaneous speaking, job interview simulation, and safety demonstrations.

For information about the VICA programs, write to:

Vocational Industrial Clubs of America
105 North Virginia Avenue
Falls Church, Virginia 22046

9 / Tools of the Trade

Hand Tools   In addition to the usual screwdrivers, wrenches, files and hammers used in all the mechanical trades, the machinist requires special precision hand instruments and tools for his work. On the following pages you will have a chance to become acquainted with the items that go into a machinist's tool kit.

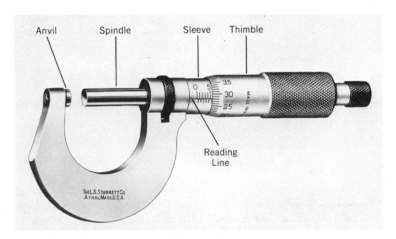

Parts of a micrometer.

The outside micrometer caliper has a range from 0 to one inch, with gradations down to ten thousandths of an inch, or hundredths of a millimeter.   (*Starrett Tools photo*)

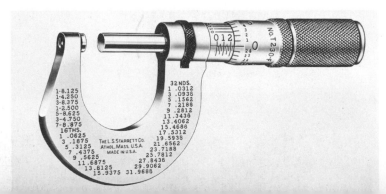

The groove micrometer can measure widths of internal or external grooves or lands. Gradations are .001-inch.

(Starrett Tools photo)

The inspector's gage has a range from 0 to 1 13/16 inch, and is graduated in 32/nds and 40ths of an inch. It is used to measure thickness of ship plates, boiler plates, etc., where measurement has to be taken through a bolt hole or small drilled hole.

(Starrett Tools photo)

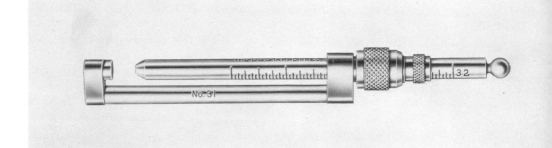

The deep throat micrometer is designed to measure steel sheets. This model has a 6-inch throat.

(Starrett Tools photo)

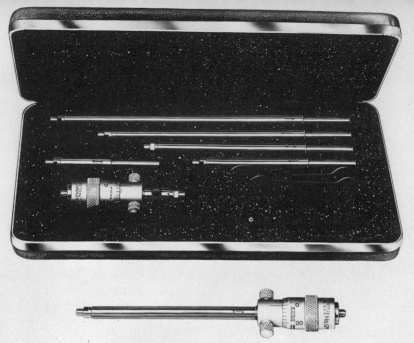

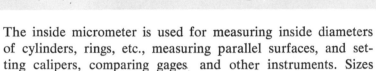

The inside micrometer is used for measuring inside diameters of cylinders, rings, etc., measuring parallel surfaces, and setting calipers, comparing gages and other instruments. Sizes range from a few inches to 32 inches in length.

(Starrett Tools photo)

Micrometer depth gages also come in many sizes. They measure holes, slots, projections to thousandths of an inch. To protect their accuracy, they are usually kept in cases when not in use.

(Starrett Tools photo)

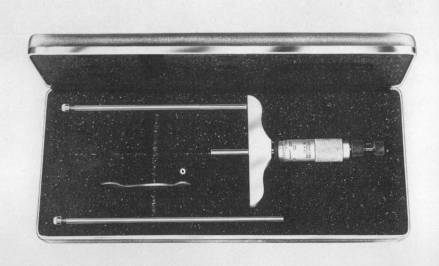

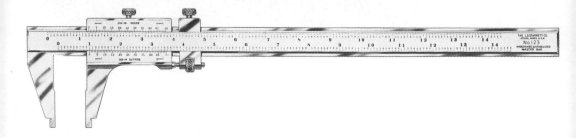

Vernier tools are highly accurate developments of the common steel measuring rule, used to determine specifications down to thousandths of an inch.

(*Starrett Tools photo*)

The combination depth and angle gage can be used as a depth gage or as a protractor, for measuring angles.

(*Starrett Tools photo*)

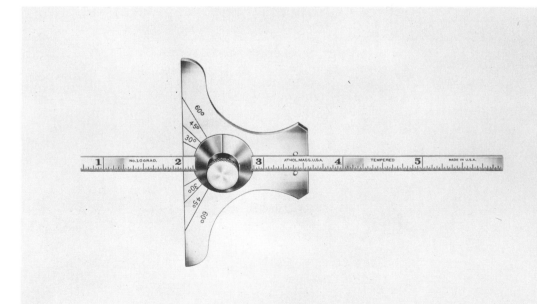

Despite all the more advanced measuring tools in his kit, the machinist's workhorse is still the old, reliable steel six-inch rule.

(Starrett Tools photo)

Screw pitch gages make it possible to determine the pitch of various threads. These gages are made up of a number of leaves, each having teeth corresponding to a certain pitch. By matching the thread with the teeth of this tool, the machinist can read the correct pitch directly from the leaf. They are made to read all standard U. S. and metric pitches.

(Starrett Tools photo)

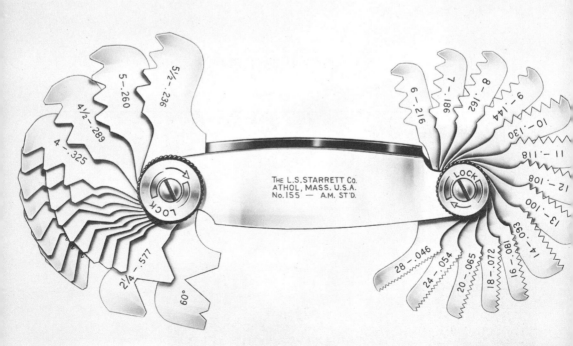

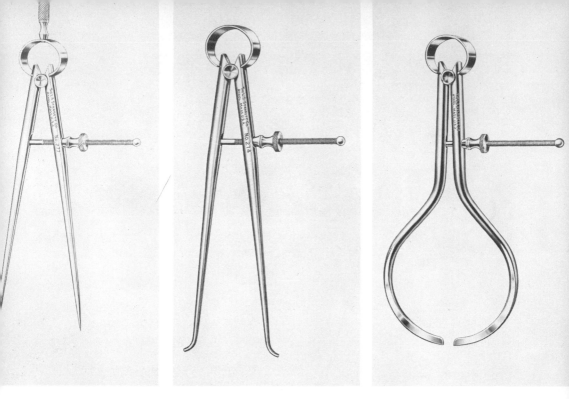

The machinist's tool kit will contain calipers of different types. They are used for such layout work as locating and testing center and laying off distance from an edge.

(*Starrett Tools photo*)

The hermaphrodite caliper is being used here to scribe a line parallel to the edge of the workpiece.

(*Starrett Tools photo*)

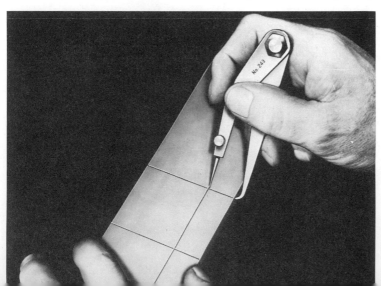

This pocket scriber is being used by a layout man to scribe a line on metal, using the edge of a hardened steel square as a guide.

(*Starrett Tools photo*)

A learner's kit for student machinists contains the following:

>   6″ combination square with center head
>   6″ flexible rule with clip
>   center gage
>   5″ divider with solid nut
>   6″ outside caliper with solid nut
>   6″ inside caliper with solid nut
>   instruction manual

(*Starrett Tools photo*)

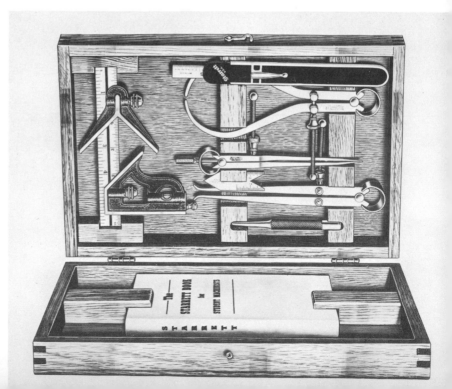

Tools of the Trade

THE BIG MACHINES

The work-life of the machinist is centered about the big, powerful machines that do the actual work of shaping the metal, or other material, to the specifications that the machinist has followed in setting up the work. Here are the machines that turn out the finished products.

The Big Machines

The massive presses are among the most powerful equipment in a machine shop.

Ever since the Bronze Age, nearly 6000 years ago, when metals were first shaped for use, people have been melting them, pouring them into molds, and pounding them into various shapes. This kind of metalworking does not involve metal cutting or removing, but rather a forming or reshaping of the material. It is similar to the type of metal forming that takes place when a nail is bent or improperly installed. The nail is then hammered into the desired position or shape. Every cook knows how to make a cake or make a jello mold. These are merely simple examples of molding non-metal substances.

Forming machines, or presses, perform the same type of forming operation. Today, machines can do in a few seconds jobs that would take the hand blacksmith hours, often days, to accomplish. In addition to metals, many other materials such as plastics can be shaped by forming machines. Many modern industries depend almost entirely on forming machines to manufacture their products.

93

OBI stamping press
(National Machine Tool Builders Association photo)

Stone saws were first used in 5000 B.C., bronze saws in 1400 B.C., and iron saws in 400 B.C. The first known file was made of iron about 100 A.D. Today, we still use saws and files mostly made of steel.

You may not see much similarity between a saw and a file, but there is one: both have a series of

94

small "teeth" used for cutting. This similarity is put to work in the milling machine, which can work both as a mechanically powered saw and as a mechanically powered file.

The main difference between the cutting edge of a hand saw or file and that of a milling machine cutter is that the teeth on the hand tools are arranged in a straight line, while those on the machine tool cutter are arranged in a circle.

There are several types of milling cutters which give the milling machine the flexibility to do a number of different jobs. Basically, however, each tooth on any milling cutter cuts a chip from the workpiece every time the cutter makes a full revolution.

The milling machine was invented by Eli Whitney in 1818. It has since become the most versatile of machine tools—and possibly the most important.

(National Machine Tool Builders Association photo)

Have you ever seen pottery being made by hand? Today, as in 2500 B.C., some artists use what is called a "potter's wheel" to spin wet clay while their hands shape the clay into a vase, jar, bottle, bowl or other object.

Almost the same thing happens to metal on a lathe. Here the "workpiece" (the metal object being worked on) is turned while a cutter is held against or moved over the workpiece to give it a new shape.

The lathe was one of the earliest machine tools developed and is still one of the most important.

(*National Machine Tool Builders Association photo*)

Planer

(National Machine Tool Builders Association photo)

We have known how to plane wood for many centuries. The principle is the same used for cutting metals with modern machine tools.

When a carpenter moves his hand plane over a piece of wood, the process is called planing. In metalworking, planing is used to achieve the same results, with the exception that the workpiece is moved across a stationary tool.

Shaping, on the other hand, refers to the cutting of metal as a result of moving the cutting tool back and forth across a stationary workpiece. This basic kind of metalworking dates back as far as 1750, or perhaps even earlier. No one is sure of the actual date of invention, or who invented it, but it has evolved as one of the basic metalworking operations.

The modern grinding machine is used to remove metal rapidly as well as to obtain a smooth surface. The grinding wheel, which may consist of any of several types of cutting materials, spins at

Grinding machine
(*National Machine Tool Builders Association photo*)

a very heavy rate of speed against the workpiece. This process may take off great quantities of metal, as the term "abrasive machine" implies. It also achieves the extra-smooth surface required in precision work.

Grinding wheel
(*National Machine Tool Builders Association photo*)

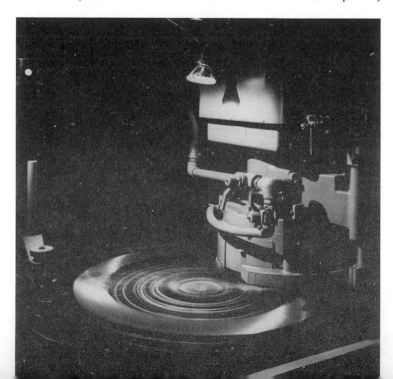

Horizontal grinder
   (*National Machine Tool Builders Association photo*)

The grinding machine shown above is a horizontal grinder.

The mechanically powered drill or drill press can perform a variety of jobs. Besides having the

Tape-controlled drilling machine
   (*National Machine Tool Builders Association photo*)

ability to cut a perfectly round hole through just about any material, the drill press can also smooth out the inside of a hole, make the hole larger, and "tap" a thread on the inside of the hole, so that a screw or bolt can be inserted.

Mechanically powered drill
(National Machine Tool Builders Association photo)

10 / Metric Conversion Tables

The United States is gradually adopting the **metric system,** the standard of weights and measures used by most of the world. This means that our system of using pounds, ounces, inches, feet and miles, pints and quarts, will give way to the international system of using kilograms, grams, millimeters, centimeters, kilometers, and liters.

For example, in the near future, when you go to a store to pick up a container of milk, you will find it marked ½ liter or liter, instead of the old pint or quart.

The most important change to the new system will be in the field of production, where all measurements and instruments will follow the new system.

Machinists will probably be among those most affected by the change. They will have to learn to think in terms of the metric system. One official of the AFL-CIO labor union says that the change-over will place a special burden on machinists. He argues that a typical machinist who buys his own tools might has to spend as much as four thousand dollars for a new set of metric-measure tools. The

101

union says that the government should help workers replace their measuring tools and instruments.

Perhaps you learned something about the metric system in school. Many states have prepared classwork material in metrics, and others are in the process of switching over.

Conversion Tables The following Metric Conversion Tables describe the metric system of weights and measures, and show how to change our common measurements to the metric system.

THE METRIC SYSTEM

The metric system is based on the **meter,** which was designed to be one ten-millionth (1/10,000,000) part of the earth's meridian quadrant, through Dunkirk and Formentera. Later investigations, however, have shown that the meter exceeds one ten-millionth part by almost one part in 6400. The value of the meter as authorized by the United States government, is 39.37 in.* The metric system was legalized by the United States Government in 1866.

The three principal units are the **meter,** the unit of length; the **liter,** the unit of capacity; and the **gram,** the unit of weight. Multiples of these are obtained by prefixing the Greek words: deka (10), hekto (100), and kilo (1000). Divisions are obtained by prefixing the Latin words: deci (1/10), centi (1/100) and milli (1/1000). Abbreviations of the multiples begin with a capital letter, and of the divisions with a small letter, as in the following tables:

METRIC CONVERSION TABLE

Millimeters	×	.03937	= Inches
Millimeters	=	25.400	× Inches
Meters	×	3.2809	= Feet
Meters	=	.3048	× Feet
Kilometers	×	.621377	= Miles
Kilometers	=	1.6093	× Miles
Square centimeters	×	.15500	= Square inches
Square centimeters	=	6.4515	× Square inches
Square meters	×	10.76410	= Square feet
Square meters	=	.09290	× Square feet
Square kilometers	×	247.1098	= Acres
Square kilometers	=	.00405	× Acres
Hectares		2.471	= Acres
Hectares	=	.4047	× Acres
Cubic centimeters	×	.061025	= Cubic inches
Cubic centimeters	=	16.3866	× Cubic inches
Cubic meters	×	35.3156	= Cubic feet
Cubic meters	=	.02832	× Cubic feet
Cubic meters	×	1.308	= Cubic yards
Cubic meters	=	.765	× Cubic yards
Liters	×	61.023	= Cubic inches
Liters	=	.01639	× Cubic inches
Liters	×	.26418	= U.S. gallons
Liters	=	3.7854	× U.S. gallons
Grams	×	15.4324	= Grains
Grams	=	.0648	× Grains
Grams	×	.03527	= Ounces, avoirdupois
Grams	=	28.3495	× Ounces, avoirdupois
Kilograms	×	2.2046	= Pounds
Kilograms	=	.4536	× Pounds
Kilograms per square centimeter	×	14.2231	= Pounds per square inch
Kilograms per square centimeter	=	.0703	× Pounds per square inch
Kilograms per cubic meter	×	.06243	= Pounds per cubic foot
Kilograms per cubic meter	=	16.01890	× Pounds per cubic foot
Metric tons (1,000 kilograms)	×	1.1023	= Tons (2,000 pounds)
Metric tons	=	.9072	× Tons (2,000 pounds)
Kilowatts	×	1.3405	= Horse-power
Kilowatts	=	.746	× Horse-power
Calories	×	3.9683	= B. T. units
Calories	=	.2520	× B. T. units

	When you know:	You can find:	If you multiply by:
LENGTH	inches	millimeters	25
	feet	centimeters	30
	yards	meters	0.9
	miles	kilometers	1.6
	millimeters	inches	0.04
	centimeters	inches	0.4
	meters	yards	1.1
	kilometers	miles	0.6
AREA	square inches	square centimeters	6.5
	square feet	square meters	0.09
	square yards	square meters	0.8
	square miles	square kilometers	2.6
	acres	square hectometers (hectares)	0.4
	square centimeters	square inches	0.16
	square meters	square yards	1.2
	square kilometers	square miles	0.4
	square hectometers (hectares)	acres	2.5
MASS	ounces	grams	28
	pounds	kilograms	0.45
	short tons	megagrams (metric tons)	0.9
	grams	ounces	0.035
	kilograme	pounds	2.2
	megagrams (metric tons)	short tons	1.1
LIQUID VOLUME	ounces	milliliters	30
	pints	liters	0.47
	quarts	liters	0.95
	gallons	liters	3.8
	milliliters	ounces	0.034
	liters	pints	2.1
	liters	quarts	1.06
	liters	gallons	0.26
TEMPERATURE	degrees Fahrenheit	degrees Celsius	5/9 (after subtracting 32)
	degrees Celsius	degrees Fahrenheit	9/5 (then add 32)

Measures of Length

10 millimeters (mm)	= 1 centimeter (cm)
10 centimeters	= 1 decimeter (dm)
10 decimeters	= 1 meter (m)
1000 meters	= 1 kilometer (km)

* Actually 39.3701″ per meter since 1 inch is officially 25.4 mm.

Measures of Area

100 sq millimeters (mm^2)	= 1 sq centimeter (cm^2)
100 sq centimeters	= 1 sq decimeter (dm^2)
100 sq decimeters	= 1 sq meter (m^2)

Measures of Volume

1000 cu millimeters (mm^3)	= 1 cu centimeter (cm^3)
1000 cu centimeters	= 1 cu decimeter (dm^3)
1000 cu decimeters	= 1 cu meter (m^3)

Measures of Capacity

10 milliliters (ml)	= 1 centiliter (cl)
10 centiliters	= 1 deciliter (dl)
10 deciliters	= 1 liter (l)

NOTE: The liter is equal to the volume occupied by 1 cubic decimeter.

Measures of Weight

10 milligrams (mg)	= 1 centigram (cg)
10 centigrams	= 1 decigram (dg)
10 decigrams	= 1 gram (g)
1000 grams	= 1 kilogram (kg)
1000 kilograms	= 1 ton (T)

NOTE: The gram is the weight of 1 cubic centimeter of pure distilled water at a temperature of 39.2 F; the kilogram is the weight of 1 liter of water; the ton is the weight of 1 cubic meter of water.

(Courtesy Alina Corporation, Plainview, New York)

Appendix A

Bureau of Apprenticeship and Training Field Offices

Alabama

Birmingham 35205
1931 Ninth Avenue S.,
South Twentieth Building

Mobile 36602
324 Federal Building

Montgomery 36104
816 Aronov Building
474 South Court Street

Alaska

Anchorage 99501
Room 46, Federal Bldg.

Arizona

Phoenix 85004
Room 2016, 1330 N. First
Street, Federal Building

Tucson 85701
130 South Scott Ave.,
Rm. 112

Arkansas

Little Rock 72201
3006 Federal Building
700 West Capital Avenue

California

Los Angeles 90012
Room 7624,
300 N. Los Angeles Street

Sacramento 95814
Room 213, 8th and Eye
Streets, Post Office Bldg.

San Diego 92101
206 Mony Building,
1927 Fifth Avenue

San Francisco 94102
Room 10457, 450 Golden
Gate Avenue

Colorado

Denver 80202
306 New Custom House
721 - 19th Street

Pueblo 81103
609 Thatcher Bldg.,
5th and Main Streets

Connecticut

Bridgeport 06603
Room 306, Federal Bldg.

Hartford 06101
303 Post Office Building,
135 High Street

New Haven 06501
State-Federal Building
746 Chapel Street, Rm. 32

Delaware

Wilmington 19801
Room 321,
Post Office Building

Florida

Jacksonville 32202
Box 35082, 400 W. Bay St.

Miami 33132
Room 1401, 41 N.E. First
Avenue

Orlando 32804
221 Executive Building,
2520 North Orange Avenue

Tallahassee 32303
Suite 418,
1309 Thomasville Road

Tampa 33602
324 Federal Building
500 Zack Street

Georgia
Atlanta 30309
Room 725, 1371 Peachtree
Street NE.

Columbus 31906
2210 Wynnton Road

Savannah 31402
326 Post Office Building

Hawaii
Honolulu 96815
Room 618, 1833 Kalakaua
Avenue

Idaho
Boise 83702
498 Post Office Building

Pocatello 83201
Suite 3, MacKenzie Building,
403 North Main Street

Illinois
Chicago 60104
(Bellwood)
413 Mannheim Road

Des Plaines 60016
2510 Dempster Street

Lansing 60438
18525 S. Torrence Avenue

Peoria 61602
319 First National Bank
Building

Rockford 61101
224 Post Office Building,
401 South Main Street

Springfield 62701
324 U.S. Post Office & Court
House, 600 East Main St.

Wood River 62095
15 East Ferguson Avenue

Indiana
Evansville 47708
Room 246 Federal Bldg.

Fort Wayne 46802
345 W. Wayne Street

Gary 46401
610 Connecticut Street

Indianapolis 46204
36 S. Pennsylvania Street

South Bend 46601
315 Whitcomb-Keller Bldg.,
224 West Jefferson Blvd.

Iowa
Davenport 52801
351 Federal Building,
U.S. Court House

Des Moines 50309
637 Federal Building,
210 Walnut Street

Kansas
Topeka 66611
320 West 33d Street

Wichita 67202
923 Beacon Building,
114 South Main Street

Kentucky
Lexington 40507
400 Nunn Building,
121 Walnut Street

Louisville 40202
Room 187-L Federal Bldg.,
600 Federal Street

Louisiana
Baton Rouge 70806
8312 Florida Avenue,
Rm. 215E

New Orleans 70113
13041 Federal Building
701 Loyola Avenue

105

Shreveport 71101
301 Medical Arts Building,
624 Travis Street

Maine
Augusta 04330
Room 101-E, Federal Bldg.

Portland 04112
Room 105, Post Office Bldg.

Maryland
Baltimore 21201
Room 1028, Federal Bldg.
31 Hopkins Plaza

Massachusetts
Boston 02203
1703A JFK Federal Bldg.,
Government Center

Lawrence 01840
Room 426, Bay State
Building, 301 Essex Street

Springfield 01103
410-412 Stearns Building,
293 Bridge Street

Worcester 01601
500 Post Office Building

Michigan
Battle Creek 49107
Battle Creek Federal Center,
74 North Washington Ave.

Detroit 48226
Room 336 U.S. Post Office
& Courthouse

Grand Rapids 49502
160 Iónia Avenue, NW.

Lansing 48933
Room 451, 106 West Allegan

Marquette 49855
232 Federal Building

Saginaw 48607
104 Federal Building

Minnesota
Duluth 55802
Room 204, Federal Building

St. Paul 55101
Room 134, Federal Building
and U.S. Court House

Mississippi
Gulfport 39501
Room 312, Gulf South Bldg.

Jackson 39201
760 Milner Building

Missouri
Kansas City 64106
2111 Federal Office Building
911 Walnut Street

St. Louis 63102
1208 Federal Building
208 North Broadway

Montana
Great Falls 59401
205 Professional Building,
510 First Avenue, North

Helena 59601
Room 1, South Annex
Power Block

Nebraska
Omaha 68102
2412 Federal Office Building,
215 North 17th Street

Nevada
Las Vegas 89101
Federal Bldg., U.S. Court
House
300 Las Vegas Blvd., South

Reno 89502
300 Booth Street

New Hampshire
Concord 03301
321 Federal Building,
55 Pleasant Street

New Jersey
New Brunswick 08901
Room 14, 96 Bayard Street

Newark 07102
970 New Federal Building

Trenton 08608
405 Federal Building
402 East State Street

New Mexico
Albuquerque 87101
517 Gold Avenue SW.

Roswell 88201
Room 149, Federal Building
5th & Richardson Street

New York
Albany 12207
406-408 New P.O. Building

Binghamton 13902
311 Post Office Building

Buffalo 14202
501 U.S. Court House,
69 Niagara Square

Hempstead, L.I. 11550
156 N. Franklin St.

New York 10007
Room 4024, 26 Federal Plaza

Rochester 14614
210 U.S. Post Office & Court
House Bldg., Church Street

Syracuse 13202
208 O'Donnell Bldg.,
321 Erie Blvd., W.

North Carolina
Charlotte 28202
415 BSR Building,
316 East Morehead Street

Greensboro 27401
P.O. Building, Box 2317

Raleigh 27605
Room 121, 1330 Saint Mary's
Street

Salisbury 28144
132 North Main Street,
Room 207

North Dakota
Fargo 58102
242 New Federal Building
653 2nd Avenue North

Ohio
Akron 54308
72 South High Street

Canton 44702
1020 Market Avenue, North

Cleveland 44199
1240 E. Ninth, Rm. 887

Cincinnati 45202
740 Federal Building

Columbus 43215
74 East Gay Street

Dayton 45402
701 Twenty-Five South Main
Bldg., 25 South Main Street

Toledo 43604
7206 Federal Office Building,
234 Summit Street

Youngstown 44501
9 W. Front Street, Room 311

Oklahoma
Oklahoma City 73102
Room 725
Post Office Building
Third & North Robinson

Tulsa 74103
Room 311 Federal Bldg.
333 W. Fourth St.

Oregon
Eugene 97401
835 Park East

Portland 97204
Room 322
310 SW. Pine St.

Pennsylvania
Altoona 16601
217 Central Trust Bldg.,
1216-18 11th Avenue

Erie 16507
316 Federal Building
Sixth and State Streets

Harrisburg 17108
770 Federal Bldg.
228 Walnut Street

Philadelphia 19107
Room 714, 1317 Filbert St.
Penn Square Bldg.

Pittsburgh 15222
1102 New Federal Building

Reading 19603
212 U.S. Post Office Building
Fifth & Washington Sts.

Scranton 18503
415 U.S. Post Office Building
Washington & Linden Streets

Rhode Island
Providence 02914
East Providence Post
Office Building

South Carolina
Charleston 29403
334 Meeting Street Room 313

Columbia 29201
Room 502-A,
901 Sumter Street

Spartanburg 29301
Room 321,
201 Magnolia Street

South Dakota
Sioux Falls 57102
Room 309, Federal Bldg.
400 S. Phillips Avenue

Tennessee
Chattanooga 37402
900 Georgia Avenue

Kingsport 37662
320 W. Center Street

Knoxville 37902
Room 232, 301 Cumberland
Avenue

Memphis 38103
214 Federal Office Bldg.
167 North Main Street

Nashville 37203
780 U.S. Court House,
801 Broad Street

Texas
Amarillo 79106
Room 218, 804 Bryan Street

Austin 78701
300 E. 8th Street

Beaumont 77704
300 Willow Street

Corpus Christi 78401
205 North Chaparral Street

Dallas 75201
Room 1003, 1416 Commerce
Street

El Paso 79901
303 N. Oregon Street

Houston 77004
2320 La Branch Street

Longview 75601
211 Earlee Building,
222-24 East Methvin St.

San Antonio 78204
651 South Main

Waco 76701
579 Westview Village

Fort Worth 76102
410 U.S. Courthouse and
Federal Bldg., 10th and
Lamarr Streets

108

Appendix A

Utah
Salt Lake City 84111
6402 Federal Building,
125 South State Street

Vermont
Burlington 05402
P.O. Box 966, Federal
Bldg., Elmwood Avenue

Virginia
Norfolk 23510
304 Allard Bldg., 102 W.
Olney Road

Richmond 23240
Room 10-021, 400 North
Eighth Street

Washington
Seattle 98104
2006 Smith Tower,
506 Second Avenue

Spokane 99201
216 Post Office Building

Tacoma 98401
412 Post Office Building

West Virginia
Charleston 25301
3011 Federal Building,
500 Quarrier Street

Clarksburg 26302
211 Post Office Building,
500 West Pike Street

Wheeling 26003
433 Federal Building
12th & Chapline Streets

Wisconsin
La Crosse 54602
211 Post Office Building

Madison 53701
Room 529, 373 Price Pl.

Milwaukee 53203
Room 160, 819 North Sixth
Street

Racine 53403
321 Arcade Building,
425 Main Street

Wyoming
Casper 82001
Room 103, 254 North
Center Street

Cheyenne 82001
Room 2015, 2120 Capital
Avenue, P.O. Box 1126

Appendix B

Civil Service Commission Offices

These are the Civil Service Offices where you can get information about opportunities for **machinist** trainees:

State and city	Area served
WASHINGTON, D.C. 20415 Civil Service Commission Bldg. 1900 E. St. NW.	District of Columbia; Charles, Montgomery, and Prince Georges counties, Md.; Arlington, Fairfax, Prince William, King George, Stafford, and Loudoun counties, Va.; Alexandria, Falls Church, and Fairfax, Va.; and overseas areas except Western Pacific area
ALABAMA Huntsville 35801 Southerland Bldg. 806 Governors Dr. SW.	Northern Alabama
Mobile 36602 First National Bank Bldg. 107 St. Francis St.	Southern Alabama (excluding Russell county) and Florida counties west of Apalachicola River (See Macon, Ga.)
ALASKA Anchorage 99051 Hill Bldg., 632 6th Ave.	Alaska
Fairbanks 99701 Fort Wainwright	Subsidiary to Anchorage
ARIZONA Phoenix 85003 Balke Bldg. 44 W. Adams St.	Arizona (except Navajo-Hopi Indian Reservations) (See Albuquerque, New Mex.)

Appendix B

State and city	Area served
ARKANSAS Little Rock 72203 923 W. Fourth St.	Arkansas (except Crittenden and Miller counties) (See Memphis, Tenn., and Dallas, Tex.)
CALIFORNIA Los Angeles 90014 Eastern Columbia Bldg. 851 S. Broadway	Kern, Los Angeles, Orange, San Luis Obispo, Santa Barbara, and Ventura counties
Long Beach 90813 1340 Pine Ave.	Subsidiary to Los Angeles
Santa Maria 93454 Rm. 207 Post Office Bldg. 120 W. Cypress St.	Subsidiary to Los Angeles
Sacramento 95814 650 Capitol Mall, Rm. 4210	California (except Lassen county) (See Reno, Nevada)
San Bernardino 92401 380 W. Court St.	Riverside and San Bernardino counties
San Diego 92101 1400 5th Ave., Suite 100	San Diego and Imperial counties
San Francisco 94102 450 Golden Gate Ave. Box 36122	San Francisco area and Central Western California
COLORADO Denver 80202 Rm. 203, Post Office Bldg. 18th and Stout Streets	Colorado
CONNECTICUT Hartford 06103 Rm. 716, Federal Bldg. 450 Main St.	Connecticut and Berkshire, Franklin, Hampden, and Hampshire counties, Mass.

111

State and city	*Area served*
DELAWARE Wilmington 19801 Post Office and Court- house 11th and King Sts.	Delaware
FLORIDA Orlando 32803 3101 Maguire Blvd.	Florida east of Apalachicola River (See Mobile, Ala.)
GEORGIA Atlanta 30303 275 Peachtree St. NE.	Northern Georgia (except Walker county) (See Memphis, Tenn.)
Macon 31201 Federal Bldg. 451 College St.	Southern Georgia; Russell county, Ala.; and Aiken county, S.C.
HAWAII Honolulu 96813 Federal Bldg.	Hawaii and Western Pacific area
IDAHO Boise 83702 Rm. 663, Fed. Bldg. U.S. Courthouse 550 W. Fort St.	Idaho
ILLINOIS Chicago 60604 Rm. 1322 219 S. Dearborn St.	Illinois (except Madison and St. Clair counties) and Scott county, Iowa (See St. Louis, Mo.)
Great Lakes 60088 Bldg. 3400, Electronics Supply Office	Subsidiary to Chicago
Rock Island 61201 Bldg. 103 Rock Island Arsenal	Subsidiary to Chicago
INDIANA Indianapolis 46204 Rm. 102 36 S. Pennsylvania St.	Indiana (except Clark, Dearborn, and Floyd counties) and Henderson county, Ky. (See Louisville, Ky., and Dayton, Ohio)

112

Appendix B

113

State and city	Area served
MINNESOTA Twin Cities 55111 Rm. 196, Federal Bldg. Ft. Snelling	Minnesota (except Clay county) and Douglas county, Wis. (See Fargo, N. Dak.)
MISSISSIPPI Jackson 39201 802 N. State St.	Mississippi
MISSOURI Kansas City 64106 Federal Bldg., Rm. 129 601 E. 12th St.	Western Missouri and Johnson, Leavenworth, and Wyandotte counties, Kans.
St. Louis 63103 Federal Bldg., Rm. 1712 1520 Market St.	Eastern Missouri and Madison and St. Clair counties, Ill.
MONTANA Helena 59601 I.B.M. Bldg. 130 Neill Ave.	Montana

NEBRASKA
Omaha 68102
Courthouse and Post
   Office Bldg.,
   Rm. 1014
215 N. 17th St.
	Nebraska and Pottawattamie county, Iowa

NEVADA Reno 89502 Fed. Bldg., Room 1139 300 Booth St.	Nevada and Lassen County, Calif.
Las Vegas 89101 300 Las Vegas Blvd. S.	Subsidiary to Reno

NEW HAMPSHIRE
Portsmouth 03803
Federal Bldg.-
   U.S. Post Office
Daniel and Penhallow
   Sts.
	New Hampshire (except Hanover and Lebanon, N.H., areas) (See Burlington, Vt.)

114

State and city	Area served
NEW JERSEY Newark 07102 Federal Bldg. 970 Broad St.	New Jersey (except Camden county) (See Philadelphia, Pa.)
NEW MEXICO Albuquerque 87101 Federal Bldg. 421 Gold Ave. S.W.	New Mexico (except Dona Ana and Otero counties) and Navajo-Hopi Indian Reservations in Arizona (See El Paso, Texas, and Phoenix, Ariz.)
NEW YORK New York 10007 Federal Bldg. 26 Federal Plaza	New York City; Long Island; and Rockland, Westchester, Orange, Putnam, and Dutchess counties
Syracuse 13202 O'Donnell Bldg. 301 Erie Blvd. W.	Northern New York
NORTH CAROLINA Raleigh 27611 310 New Bern Ave. Fed. Office Bldg.	North Carolina
NORTH DAKOTA Fargo 58102 Rm. 200, Federal Bldg. and Post Office 657 Second Ave.	North Dakota and Clay county, Minn.
OHIO Cleveland 44199 New Federal Bldg. 1240 E. 9th St.	Northern Ohio
Dayton 45402 Knott Bldg. 21 E. 4th St.	Southern Ohio (excluding Belmont, Jefferson, and Lawrence counties) and Dearborn county, Ind., and Boone, Campbell, and Kenton counties, Ky. (See Charleston, W. Va.)
Cincinnati 45202 Rm. 1523 Federal Office Bldg. 550 Main St.	Subsidiary to Dayton

115

State and city	*Area served*
OKLAHOMA Oklahoma City 73102 210 NW. 6th St.	Oklahoma
OREGON Portland 97204 319 SW. Pine St.	Oregon and Clark counties, Wash.
PENNSYLVANIA Philadelphia 19102 128 N. Broad St.	Eastern Pennsylvania and Camden county, N.J.
Pittsburgh 15222 Federal Bldg. 1000 Liberty Ave.	Central and Western Pennsylvania
PUERTO RICO Hato Rey 00917 Pan Am Bldg. 255 Ponce de Leon Ave.	Puerto Rico and Virgin Islands
RHODE ISLAND Providence 02903 Federal Bldg. and Post Office Kennedy Plaza	Rhode Island and Barnstable, Bristol, Dukes, and Nantucket counties, Mass.
SOUTH CAROLINA Charleston 29403 Federal Office Bldg. 334 Meeting St.	South Carolina (except Aiken county) (See Macon, Ga.)
SOUTH DAKOTA Rapid City 57701 Dusek Bldg., 919 Main St. Rm. 118	South Dakota
TENNESSEE Memphis 38103 Federal Office Bldg. 167 N. Main St.	Tennessee and Crittenden county, Ark., Christian county, Ky., and Walker county, Ga.

116

Appendix B

117

State and city	*Area served*
WASHINGTON Seattle 98104 Federal Office Bldg. 1st Ave. and Madison St.	Washington (except Clark county) (See Portland, Oreg.)
Bremerton 98314 511 Burwell St.	Subsidiary to Seattle
WEST VIRGINIA Charleston 25301 Federal Bldg. 500 Quarrier St.	West Virginia and Belmont, Jefferson, and Lawrence counties, Ohio, and Boyd county, Ky.
WISCONSIN Milwaukee 53203 Rm. 215 161 W. Wisconsin Ave.	Wisconsin (except Douglas county) (See Twin Cities, Minn.)
WYOMING Cheyenne 82001 Rm. 108 1805 Capitol Ave.	Wyoming

Appendix C

State Apprenticeship Agencies

Arizona Apprenticeship Council
1623-B West Adams
Phoenix, Ariz. 85007

Division of Apprenticeship
  Standards
Department of Industrial Relations
305 Golden Gate Ave.
San Francisco, Calif. 94102

Colorado Apprenticeship Council
Industrial Commission Offices
200 E. Ninth Ave.
Denver, Colo. 80203

Apprentice Training Division
Labor Department
200 Folly Brook Blvd.
Wethersfield, Conn. 06109

Delaware State Apprenticeship and
  Training Council
Department of Labor and Industry
506 W. 10th St.
Wilmington, Del. 19801

District of Columbia Apprenticeship
  Council
Room 329
555 Pennsylvania Ave., NW.
Washington, D.C. 20212

Department of Apprenticeship
Florida Industrial Commission
Caldwell Building
Tallahassee, Fla. 32304

Apprenticeship Division
Department of Labor and Industrial
  Relations
825 Mililani St.
Honolulu, Hawaii 98613

Kansas Apprenticeship Council
Department of Labor
401 Topeka Blvd.
Topeka, Kan. 66603

Kentucky State Apprenticeship
  Council
Department of Labor
Frankfort, Ky. 40601

Division of Apprenticeship
Department of Labor
State Capitol Annex
Baton Rouge, La. 70804

Maine Apprenticeship Council
Department of Labor and Industry
State Office Building
Augusta, Maine 04330

Maryland Apprenticeship and
  Training Council
Department of Labor and Industry
State Office Building
Baltimore, Md. 21201

Division of Apprentice Training
Department of Labor and Industries
State Office Building
Boston, Mass. 02202

Division of Voluntary
  Apprenticeship
Department of Labor and Industry
110 State Office Building
St. Paul, Minn. 55101

Montana State Apprenticeship
  Council
Department of Labor and Industry
Room 417, Mitchell Building
Helena, Mont. 59601

Nevada Apprenticeship Council
Department of Labor
Capitol Building
Carson City, Nev. 89701

New Hampshire Apprenticeship
  Council
Department of Labor
State House Annex
Concord, N. H. 13301

New Mexico Apprenticeship
  Council
Labor and Industrial Commission
1010 National Building
Albuquerque, N. M. 87101

Bureau of Apprentice Training
Department of Labor
The Campus, Building No. 12
Albany, N. Y. 12226

Division of Apprenticeship Training
Department of Labor
Raleigh, N. C. 27602

Ohio State Apprenticeship Council
Department of Industrial Relations
220 Parsons Ave.
Columbus, Ohio 43215

Oregon State Apprenticeship
  and Training Council
Bureau of Labor
State Office Building
Portland, Ore. 97201

Pennsylvania Apprenticeship and
  Training Council
Department of Labor and Industry
Labor and Industry Building
Harrisburg, Pa. 17120

Apprenticeship Division
Department of Labor
424 Barbosa Ave.
Hato Rey, P. R. 00917

Rhode Island Apprenticeship
  Council
Department of Labor
235 Promenade St.
Providence, R. I. 02908

Utah Apprenticeship Council
431 South Sixth East, No. 225
Salt Lake City, Utah 84102

Vermont Apprenticeship Council
Department of Industrial Relations
State Office Building
Montpelier, Vt. 05602

Division of Apprenticeship Training
Department of Labor and Industry
P.O. Box 1814
Richmond, Va. 23214

Director of Apprenticeship and
  Training
Department of Labor
Christiansted, St. Croix, V.I. 00820

120

Appendix C

Apprenticeship Division
Department of Labor and Industries
315 East 5th Ave.
Olympia, Wash. 98501

Division of Apprentice Training
Department of Industry, Labor and
  Human Relations
P.O. Box 2209
Madison, Wis. 53701

Glossary

Abrasion: The process of reducing material by grinding instead of cutting with tools.

Abrasive: Crushed sharp crystals of grinding material used in the form of grinding wheels, polishing cloth and lapping powder.

Accessory: A mechanical part which need not be a part of the machine with which it is to be used, but does permit better performance or more versatility.

Adapter: Any device that serves to connect or fit together two parts of an apparatus.

Anneal: To heat a metal piece to its critical temperature and then allow it to cool slowly, reducing brittleness.

Anvil: An iron or steel block on which forging is done.

Assembly: The finished separate pieces put together according to the assembly drawing.

Assembly drawing: A drawing which shows all the parts of a structure, but does not include the dimensions of the detail drawings.

Bench hand: The worker who makes and may fit parts by hand. A qualified bench hand should have approximately the same training time as an all-around machinist.

Bench work: Work which is done at the bench or vise, rather than lathe or machine work.

Bit: The cutting tool for a lathe.

Blueprint: A plan or drawing made by printing on sensitized paper, or any detailed plan.

Boring: The process of enlarging a hole to a specified dimension.

Broach: To finish the inside of a hole to a shape other than round with a cutting tool.

Burnish: To polish to a smooth finish by working a smooth tool against moving or revolving surfaces.

Burr: The rough, usually sharp edge left on metal after a cutting or shearing operation, or the act of removing a burr.

Calibrate: To graduate a measuring instrument into appropriate units, either metric or standard.

Caliper: A machinist tool which is made in two basic designs: the *inside* caliper for measuring the inside diameter of holes, the *outside* for measuring circular work on the outside diameter.

Chip: To cut or clean metal with a cold chisel, or a piece of metal removed from the workpiece by a cutting tool.

Depth gage: A gage used for measuring the depth or holes and recessed portions of the work.

Die stamping: A piece formed or cut out by a die.

Dividers: Compasses used for measuring or setting off distances, by scratching or "scribing" lines on metal surfaces.

Drill press: A geared, power-driven machine tool used for drilling holes in metal.

Dry grinding: Grinding operations which do not use water or coolants.

Edging machine: A machine used in sheet metal work to fold over the edges of sheet metal. It is also called an "adjustable bar folder."

Engine lathe: The basic lathe used for general machine work. It was originally powered by a steam engine.

Face: To machine a flat surface on a metal piece by means of a machine tool.

Forming: The operations necessary to shape metal to a desired form. It does not intentionally cut or change the thickness of the metal.

Gage: An instrument for measuring. Also spelled gauge.

Hand tools: Tools that may be held in the hand. In the machine shop, tools are basically divided into hand tools and machine tools.

Inspection gages: A variety of gages, either of standard or special design, used to check the accuracy of finished work.

Jig: A fixture for locating, holding the work, and guiding the cutting tool in its operations.

Knurl: To roughen or indent a turned surface such as a knob or handle, to produce a better hand grip.

Lap: A soft metal surface impregnated with fine abrasive for use in polishing operations.

Glossary

Layout: The process of planning or laying out a piece of work; marking the material to be machined, to serve as a guide in the machining operation.

Machine control unit: The equipment in numerical control systems which controls operation of the machine(s).

Machine drawing: A mechanical drawing of a machine or machine parts, which include dimensions and other information necessary for its manufacture.

Machine language (a term in numerical control): The set of symbols, characters, or signs, and the rules for using them, which conveys to a computer the instructions or information to be processed.

Machining: The operations performed on metal by machine tools.

Magnetic tape: The tape which can store information and instructions in a numerical control system.

Micrometer: A device attached to a measuring instrument to allow precise adjustments or measurements.

Numerical control: The technique of controlling a machine or process using tapes and automatic controls.

Plane: To smooth or machine with a planer; or, any flat or uncurved surface.

Programmer: The person who prepares the planned

125

sequence of events for the operation of a numerically controlled machine tool.

Rate of Speed: In machine work, the rate of speed is expressed in revolutions per minute or in feet per minute.

Scribe: To draw a line on the work with a scriber or other sharp-pointed hand tool.

Tachometer: A device for indicating the speed of rotation.

Tolerance: The total permissible amount by which a dimension may vary above or below a specified size.

Turret lathe: A production lathe with a revolving tool head which holds several tools and makes possible a rapid succession of operations.

Vernier: A movable auxiliary scale used to obtain fractional parts of a fixed scale's subdivisions.

Working drawing: A drawing which provides the necessary information to make and assemble a mechanism.

Working gages: A term applied to gages used by workers as distinguished from gages used by inspectors, or master gages, used to check other instruments.

(Definitions excerpted from "Dictionary of Metalworking Terms" published by Advance Book Publishing Company, Cincinnati, Ohio.)

Index